JOURNEY TO HEAVEN

Other Books by Leila Leah Bronner

From Eve to Esther: Rabbinic Reconstructions of Biblical Women

Stories of Biblical Mothers: Maternal Power in the Hebrew Bible

Biblical Personalities and Archaeology

The Stories of Elijah and Elisha

Sects and Separation During the Second Jewish Commonwealth

Leila Leah Bronner

Journey to Heaven

*Exploring Jewish Views
of the Afterlife*

Urim Publications
Jerusalem · New York

Journey to Heaven: Exploring Jewish Views of the Afterlife
by Leila Leah Bronner

Copyright © 2011 by Leila Leah Bronner

Book design by Ariel Walden

Printed in Israel
First Edition

ISBN 978-965-524-047-4

Urim Publications
P.O.Box 52287
Jerusalem 91521 Israel

Lambda Publishers, Inc.
527 Empire Blvd.
Brooklyn, NY 11225 U.S.A.
Tel: 718-972-5449, fax: 718-972-6307

www.UrimPublications.com

For my father

ᚷ   Rabbi Yitzchok (Isaac) Amsel ז"ל

A great Talmudic and Kabbalistic scholar who devoted his life to making Torah great and glorious   *(Isaiah 42:21)*

Contents

Preface

MY INTEREST IN the next world awakened during my career as a scholar in Bible and Jewish studies. Often, when preparing for lectures, I would note that many scriptural commentators insisted that the Bible contained no references to the afterlife until the book of Daniel. This gave me pause on the spiritual level. I couldn't understand how Israel could be described as "the people of God" and at the same time believe that everything came to a halt with one's death. It also caused my intellectual antennae to quiver and piqued me to take a closer look at the subject as a textual matter. Couldn't there be other biblical passages that alluded, however obliquely, to the question of what happens after death?

When I began to explore this matter, I discovered a number of allusions to a life hereafter in the Hebrew Bible. That led me to pursue the question of the afterlife throughout Jewish textual history: in the writings of the Second Temple period; in the rabbinic texts of the Mishnah and Talmud; in medieval and mystical works; and in the commentaries and writings of the modern era. I found that Judaism has a great deal to say about what happens after we die. Eventually it became important to me to set down those ideas in a systematic way, and it is from that impulse that this book arises.

Some of the ideas in this book are based on lectures I delivered at the American Academy of Religion/Society of Biblical Literature and in various study circles, and one chapter is based on a paper published in *Dor L'Dor* (now called the *Jewish Bible Quarterly*). My ideas have evolved as I have worked on this book; consequently, those parts of the text based on earlier presentations have been thoroughly reworked from any earlier format.

Unless otherwise cited, translations of biblical texts have been taken from the latest Jewish Publication Society version of the *Tanakh* or the Artscroll *Tanach*; the Mishnah from the Danby edition; and excerpts from the Babylonian Talmud and *Midrash Rabbah* from the Soncino editions, with some Talmud texts taken from the Schottenstein translations. At times I have provided my own translations, which are indicated in the notes. Transliteration of Hebrew terms follows the simplified style of the *Encyclopaedia Judaica*, with the following exceptions: this book uses *h* for both ח (*het*) and ה (*heh*); *kh* for כ (*khaf*); and *k* for both כ (*kaf*) and ק (*kuf*).

A number of friends and colleagues have been most kind in their readiness to discuss aspects of the work with me: Michael Berenbaum, editor of the new edition of the *Encyclopaedia Judaica*; art historian Marcia Reines Josephy; and Bezalel Porten and Moshe Herr, emeritus Jewish history professors at Hebrew University. I want to acknowledge Tzvi Mauer, publisher, and the entire Urim staff for working tirelessly to get this book into print. Thanks also go to Deborah Silver, who typed the first draft, to Ellen Jaffe-Gill, who provided invaluable support in researching and drafting the initial manuscript, and to Bonny V. Fetterman, my independent editor, who worked closely with me in bringing the manuscript into its final form.

Finally, I want to thank my husband, Rabbi Joseph Bronner, for his support and encouragement in this project as in so many other endeavors in my life.

Leila Leah Bronner

Los Angeles
January 2011

Introduction

I HAVE OFTEN HEARD people say that Judaism is a faith concerned with life in this world, not a religion that dwells on what we might expect beyond the grave. For some, this orientation is an asset: Judaism attaches a paramount value to the reality of this life and its teachings are directed at ameliorating this world. Yet every culture – and probably every individual – has at some point asked: what happens after we die? Is it possible that only Judaism has not allowed itself to speculate on this most intimate and most universal question? For me, this view of Judaism not only implies a lack of spiritual and religious imagination, but it also ignores rich sources of Jewish thought and sacred writings going back hundreds of years that discuss and describe views of the hereafter. In my own experience, I did not have to go back that far to encounter this belief.

I was born in Czechoslovakia and came to America as a child with my parents, who were among the last Jews to escape the Nazis in the 1930s. My father was a *rebbe* – a hasidic rabbi and a Lurianic kabbalist – who often spoke about the meaning of life and its connection to death. He conceived of *olam ha-ba* (the World to Come) as a beautiful place, and said we should not fear death because it too has a meaning and a purpose. As a young child, I once asked him, "Tati, if *olam ha-ba* is such a wonderful place, why don't we go there now?" My father, not realizing that the question came from spiritual inquiry and not from heretical leanings, was not amused.

The World to Come was also a real concept to my mother, who referred to it in Yiddish (instead of Hebrew) as *yenner velt* (the next world). A song she used to sing to me about the next world contained this lyric: *In yenner velt iz nisht du kayn gelt / Urem und reich iz dort gleikh* ("In the next world, there is no money; rich and poor are equal"). This vision of a just, equitable World to Come was a compelling and hopeful image for me as a child growing up in the shadow of war and poverty, albeit in the relative safety of Brooklyn. Though I was not yet aware of the tragedy unfolding in Europe, my parents surely were.

In what was, I suppose, an unusual choice for a girl from a hasidic family, I pursued my interest in Jewish studies in the academic world. I earned my doctorate in ancient Semitic languages in South Africa, where I moved with my husband after our marriage, eventually becoming Professor of Bible and Jewish History at the University of Witwatersrand in Johannesburg. It is not surprising, therefore, that my inquiry into Jewish views of the afterlife began with the Hebrew Bible.

I have long taken issue with the general consensus among scholars that the Bible does not deal in any significant way with the concept of an afterlife. The conventional wisdom has been that because the Bible concerns itself primarily with community and national continuity, stressing corporate Israel and the covenant promise of Israel's survival as a people, it has little, if anything, to say about the fate of the individual after death. I always found this hard to believe. After all, people wonder what happens after death today, so why shouldn't the same be true of people at the time of the Bible?

This initial query set me on a long path that has resulted in this book. During my research, I discovered that some scholars do hold the view that there are allusions in the Hebrew Bible to a belief in some sort of hereafter. Moving forward in Jewish history, I found that successive generations of Jewish thinkers and writers, rabbis, and philosophers have explored, explained, and elaborated on the ideas behind these biblical hints. As a result, there now exists a fascinating body of material in the Jewish tradition as a whole that deals with what happens after death, albeit not in any systematic or dogmatic fashion.

Because a number of renowned scholars as well as popular writers have addressed themselves to this subject, it is fair to ask why I felt it necessary to add another book to the stack. First, I wanted to present some of the actual texts from Jewish tradition rather than offer them in paraphrase. By including clear, understandable translations of writings that concern the afterlife, I feel that readers will be better equipped to form their own judgments about the material.

My second aim is to assist the reader in seeing how the body of Jewish thought about the afterlife has grown throughout the ages. For this reason I have kept to a chronological framework: the Hebrew Bible, the post-biblical writings of the Apocrypha and Pseudepigrapha, rabbinic texts such as the Mishnah and Talmud, writings of both rationalist philosophers of the medieval period, the Kabbalah and mystical movements, and theological thinking in modernity. This historical structure will enable the reader to follow the development of central themes (resurrection, immortality, reincarnation, and the World to Come) as they emerge and are interpreted over time. One final chapter is entirely devoted to the Messiah, a theme that is closely linked to Jewish thinking about the afterlife and has its own fascinating evolution over time.

Third, I have tried wherever possible to describe the social and historical context out of which Jewish teachings on the afterlife arose. It is impossible to appreciate fully the scope and significance of an idea without some sense of the circumstances that gave rise to it. My goal has been to create an accessible guide in narrative form to the many-faceted, often obscure realm of Jewish thought about the afterlife.

The structure of the book, then, is as follows:

1. The Bible, where we consider the arguments for and against belief in a hereafter during this period. As we shall see, there are allusions, and sometimes more than allusions, to a shadowy realm after death where the deceased have some form of existence.

2. The Apocrypha and Pseudepigrapha, which, though not included in the Hebrew Bible, nevertheless played an important role in Jewish history in the Second Temple period. Here we encounter a large body of literature speculating about life after death, heaven, hell, and judgment. This literature offers not only discussions of resurrection but also introduces the theme of the immortality of the soul.

3. The Mishnah, the great interpretive work of the early rabbis, which speaks at length about World to Come and how to be worthy of entering

it. We will see that the rabbis have a clear preference for a doctrine of resurrection over immortality and consider why this is so.

4. The Talmud, the work of the later generations of Jewish rabbis, in which the laws of the Mishnah are interpreted and expanded. The themes of resurrection and the World to Come are closely analyzed and developed. We will also see how this generation of rabbis discusses the relationship between the body and the soul.

5. The great Jewish philosophers of the medieval period from the tenth to fifteenth centuries who wrote about faith and reason, including Sa'adiah Gaon, Judah Halevi, Maimonides, and Nahmanides. Here we will encounter the heated "Maimonidean controversy" and Maimonides' own attempt to defend his beliefs in both immortality and bodily resurrection.

6. The Jewish mystics of the tenth to sixteenth centuries, in whose writings we see the influence of Kabbalah on views of the hereafter. In this chapter we will trace the development of the Jewish doctrine of reincarnation, which reaches its fullest expression in the Lurianic Kabbalah. We will also examine how the popular movement of Hasidism adopted and adapted the ideas of Lurianic Kabbalah.

7. The challenge posed by modernity to Jewish life and theology, including ideas about the afterlife. This chapter will survey the various liturgical changes in denominational prayer books. It will also explore the revival of interest in the afterlife in the postmodern age.

8. A historical discussion of the Messiah from biblical times to the present. We will examine how rabbis and philosophers across the generations have viewed this central concept in Jewish doctrine and its relationship to the afterlife.

Finally, whatever insights I bring to the discussion of this subject derive from the fact that I have had the privilege of living in two worlds of Jewish scholarship. The academic disciplines I have studied have given me the tools for scholarly research and the distance for critical study. At the same time, my exposure to traditional Jewish learning from sacred texts has given me an emotional proximity to this material and respect for the beliefs that have sustained the Jewish people.

It is my hope that this book will help readers understand Jewish perspectives on a subject that has been a preoccupation of humankind from generation to generation. I also hope that in discovering the variety of perspectives on matters of the hereafter, readers will experience some of the joy and excitement that I had in making this journey.

The Hebrew Bible:
Glimpses of Immortality

> ✿ *Enoch walked with God; then he was no more,*
> *for God took him.* (*Genesis 5:24*)

WHAT DID THE people of ancient Israel believe about the hereafter? Did they entertain a hope for a continued existence beyond the grave and what, if anything, did they imagine that to be? When Enoch "walked with God, then was no more," where did God take him?

From the beginning of civilization, people have made great efforts to pierce the veil of death and discover what lies beyond this life, yet until quite recently many biblical scholars maintained that the Hebrew Bible contains no substantial evidence of any interest or belief in life beyond death.[1] Since references to life after death in the Hebrew Bible are few, they assumed that life after death was not an important concept to ancient Israelites compared to tenets such as monotheism and the mandate to love one's neighbor as oneself. Numerous passages in the Bible suggest that the circle of life is closed by death and that there is no life beyond the grave. These verses seem to indicate that when the life of the body is over, nothing else remains:

> We must all die; we are like water that is poured out on
> the ground and cannot be gathered up. (2 Samuel 14:14)

> As a cloud fades away, so whoever goes down to Sheol
> does not come up. He returns no more to his home; his
> place does not know him.　　　　　　　　　(Job 7:9–10)

> Since the living know they will die, but the dead know
> nothing: they have no more recompense, for even the
> memory of them has died . . . .　　　　　(Ecclesiastes 9:5)

To contend, however, that the Bible contains no substantial evidence of a belief in life beyond death is to miss the subtle references in various biblical texts that propose an alternative belief, one that does not accept the finality of death but postulates some kind of continuity beyond the grave. Even those scholars who deny that ancient Israelites believed in life after death agree that the book of Daniel takes an unambiguous stand on the subject:

> And many of those who sleep in the dust of the earth will
> awake, some to eternal life and some to reproaches and
> everlasting abhorrence. And the wise will be radiant like
> the bright expanse of sky, and those who lead the many to
> righteousness [will shine] like the stars forever and ever.
> 　　　　　　　　　　　　　　　　　　　(Daniel 12:2–3)

While this passage by no means gives a full description of resurrection, it clearly affirms that a divine power will bring the dead back to life at some future time. Only the righteous, it says, will rise to eternal life, while the wicked will descend to eternal damnation. Furthermore, two types of people qualify as candidates for everlasting life – those who are wise and those who teach righteousness to many.

The book of Daniel is of relatively late origin. Still, it seems strange that the idea of life after death would suddenly spring forth, fully formed, with no precedents. Did these verses from Daniel occur in isolation, or can we find traces of this belief in earlier parts of the Bible?

First, let us note that most cultures surrounding ancient Israel believed in some continuity of existence after death. The people of ancient Israel could not help but be aware of these beliefs, whether they were influenced by these cultures or not.

Archaeological and other evidence displays for us the power of the ancient Egyptians' belief in total continuity between life and death. Theirs was a culture that was greatly preoccupied with the subject. This explains their practice of embalming, since the body was presumed to be still necessary for use once its owner had died. Rulers and potentates were buried in pyramids along with their servants (or statues of their servants) as well as food to sustain them on their after-death journeys.

Mesopotamian and Ugaritic literatures also record stories of heroes who journey beyond the grave. On a practical level, family graves were tended by relatives who provided the deceased with sustenance. At Ras Shamra, where the Ugaritic texts were found, excavations show pipes leading down into the graves so that the dead could receive water.

The impact of these surrounding cultures on ancient Israelite practice is evident in some of the finds in excavations at Megiddo and Hazor. Artifacts such as storage jars found at ancient burial sites indicate that the living continued to worry about the dead and made efforts to provide them with sustenance. The phenomenon of tomb openings found at several sites further suggests that people performed rituals connected with the dead.[2] If this is so, it must be at least arguable that some sort of belief in the afterlife did exist. With that in mind, let's turn back to the text of the Bible itself.

The Hebrew Bible does contain elements and allusions that indicate the presence of such a belief. The allusions are quite subtle and spread over a large number of texts spanning a wide expanse of time. Nonetheless, taken together, they do show a belief in an afterlife existence.

𓂀 SHEOL, THE BIBLICAL UNDERWORLD

The Bible frequently alludes to a place of the dead called Sheol, commonly translated as "the underworld." Supposedly, upon death, one descended to an underworld abode in the depths of the earth where the dead were gathered with their kin. Sheol is referred to more than sixty-five times in the Hebrew Bible, and the multiplicity of other metaphoric names for Sheol indicates its role in the popular imagination. For example, it is also described as "the Pit" and "the hidden place."[3]

The origin or etymology of Sheol is obscure. Most scholars think it comes from the Hebrew root *sh-'-l*, meaning "to ask." Curiously, this would lend weight to the prohibition against conjuring up the dead to ask for their counsel in the book of Leviticus: "Do not turn to ghosts and do not *inquire of* familiar spirits" (19:31) and likewise, the prohibition in Deuteronomy: "Let no one be found among you who is a soothsayer, a diviner ... or one who *inquires* of the dead" (18:11). From these prohibitions it follows that there must have been some kind of practice of consulting with the dead, though it is unclear how common it was in ancient Israel. An extraordinary example of such a consultation takes place in 1 Samuel 28, when King Saul visits the Witch of En-dor on the eve of battle against the Philistines and persuades her to bring the prophet Samuel back from the dead.

What was Sheol like? First, it is clear that Sheol is the realm of those who are no longer living. This is shown in the dramatic confrontation between Moses and Korah (Numbers 16:30), in which God determines that Moses and Aaron are the true leaders of the Israelites. Korah, who heads the evil rebellion, goes down alive into Sheol together with his clan, meaning that they were forcefully taken from the land of the living. Sheol is also regarded as being the deepest, darkest place in the world. Job describes it as "the land of deepest gloom / A land whose light is darkness / All gloom and disarray, whose light is like darkness" (Job 10:21–22). Numerous psalms use Sheol or the Pit as a metaphor for being in a place of extreme darkness, as in Ps. 88:7: "You have put me at the bottom of the Pit / In the darkest places, in the depths." In addition, the prophet Samuel, summoned from Sheol at King Saul's request, is said to have been "brought up," which would reinforce the idea of his having been in some kind of nether place.

In Sheol, most of the differences that existed in life disappear: workers rest, and prisoners do not hear the taskmaster's voice. Small and great are there alike (Job 3:17). Yet it appears that the inhabitants of Sheol have some kind of nebulous existence. The dead who inhabit Sheol are sometimes called *refa'im,* "ghosts." Although the Hebrew root *r-f-'* usually connotes healing, here it suggests weakness, as if the dead are mere shadows of the people they once were. The various occurrences of the term in the Bible are not enough to tell us very much about the *refa'im,* but we do know that they "chirp" (Isaiah 29:4) and sometimes they maintain their earthly status. Thus, in Isaiah 14, we find that when a king goes down to Sheol, he is greeted by other kings who have been enthroned there:

> Sheol below you astir to greet your coming, rousing for
> you the shades of all earth's chieftains, raising from their
> thrones all the kings of the nations.　　(Isaiah 14:9)

It would seem, then, that although differences among ordinary people are erased in Sheol, kings remain kings even after death!

The psalms mention Sheol in several contexts. It is notable, first of all, that it is a place where the dead are powerless to praise or access God's goodness:

> There is no praise of you among the dead.
> In Sheol, who can acclaim you?　　(Psalms 6:6)

> The dead cannot praise the Lord,
> Nor any who go down into silence.　　(Psalms 115:17)

God, however, apparently can reach Sheol:

> Where can I escape from your spirit?
> Where can I flee from your presence?
> If I ascend to heaven, you are there,
> If I descend to Sheol, you are there too.　　(Psalm 139:8)

Finally, references to Sheol suggest the belief that after death, one joined the previously deceased members of one's family, as is shown by Abraham's purchase of the Cave of Machpelah as a family tomb (Genesis 23). Consequently, it was critical to be buried with one's ancestors. In this context, it is revealing to consider the common terminology describing the deaths of the patriarchs and matriarchs as being "gathered to one's people." This idiom is used to describe the deaths, or incipient deaths, of Abraham (Genesis 25:8), Ishmael (Genesis 25:17), Isaac (Genesis 35:29), Jacob (Genesis 49:33), Aaron (Numbers 20:29), and Moses (Numbers 27:13). David is described as "sleeping with his fathers" (1 Kings 2:5). The importance placed on being buried with kin suggests that there must have been a basic belief in some kind of existence after death.

⚘ HINTS OF RESURRECTION

All the texts on Sheol suggest some nebulous form of existence after death, but is there any notion of deliverance from the shady realm of Sheol itself? Resurrection, briefly defined, is the belief that in the future the dead will rise from their graves, bringing about a revival of the whole person, body and soul.[4] The resurrection motif in the Hebrew Bible is suggested in a number of ways that we will now proceed to explore.

Death and Life

The Song of Moses, the great leader's final address to the Israelites before they enter the Promised Land, quotes God as saying:

> I deal death and give life;
> I wound and I will heal;
> None can deliver from My hand. (Deut. 32:39)

The arrangement of the key words – death first, followed by life – suggests a resurrection motif. The same pattern is found in the Song of Hannah:

> The Lord deals death and gives life,
> Casts down into Sheol and raises up. (1 Sam. 2:6)

This text seems to suggest, at least on a poetic level, that resurrection from Sheol is possible. In using this word order – to "deal death," then "give life" – rather than vice versa, this verse points to a time after the earthly life of the body when God will infuse the dead with the vitality they had when living.

The context of both of these verses is also significant. In the Song of Moses, the surrounding text recalls the loving care shown by God to his people. The author's confidence in God's power is then expressed by way of the resurrection motif and the theme of healing and repair. In the Song of Hannah, the power of God is again the central theme; the surrounding verses triumphantly portray a series of dramatic reversals of power and fortune. Death, as one element of these reversals, is clearly not viewed as a permanent state.

A similar theme is reflected in Psalm 16:

> For you will not abandon me to Sheol
> Or let your faithful one see the Pit.
> You will teach me the path of life.
> In your presence is perfect joy;
> Delights are ever in your right hand.   (Psalm 16:10–11)

Here it is stated that God is able to rescue his people from the pit of Sheol and allow them to praise him in the presence of the living. Once again, we see the "death, then life" pattern that possibly indicates an allusion to resurrection.[5]

Prophetic Narratives

The Elijah and Elisha narratives in 1 and 2 Kings are set in the Northern Kingdom of Israel in the ninth century B.C.E. While these prophetic narratives differ in linguistic structure and style from the poetry cited above, they too deal with the subject of resurrection. Both the prophet Elijah and Elisha, his successor, are credited with bringing a dead child back to life. Even though the child's revival might suggest resuscitation rather than resurrection, their prayers invoke the divine power to transform death to life.

Some scholars see in these stories the influences of neighboring cultures. The earliest Ugaritic texts attribute similar powers to the goddess Anat. She promises eternal life to the youth Aqht who mockingly expresses doubt in her ability to do this. She responds angrily by killing him, although it is suggested that she then goes on to revive him:

> And the maiden Anat replied:
> Ask for life, O Aqht the youth,
> Ask for life and I will give it to you,
> For deathlessness and I will bestow it on thee.
> I'll make thee count years with Baal.
> With sons of El shalt thou count months.
> Even as Baal when he gives life,
> Entertains the living . . .
> So also I will give life to Aqht the youth.
>
> (2 Aqht VI, 25–33)

The author of the stories of Elijah and Elisha is likely to have known of these texts as well as the belief that Baal, the chief Ugarit male god, was capable of reviving those he killed. Indeed, the stories are set against the wider background of an ideological struggle between Elijah and Elisha on the one hand and the prophets of Baal on the other. It is perhaps no accident that Elijah and Elisha are both credited with the kind of miracles that the surrounding cultures would attribute to Baal. By putting these miracles under the control of the two prophets of God, the author sends a clear polemical message about God's power and Baal's impotence.[6]

The dramatic story presenting the physical revival of a child by the prophet Elijah is set in the context of strife and famine in the days of King Ahab (875–854 B.C.E.) and his consort, Queen Jezebel. Elijah, having antagonized the royal court with his moral chastisement, is forced to flee for his life, and finds refuge at the home of the poor widow of Zarephath. Meanwhile, the widow's child falls sick until there is no longer any breath/soul (*neshamah*) remaining in him (I Kings 17:17). After Elijah prayed fervently to God, "the child's life returned to his body, and he revived" (I Kings 17:22). The prophet then said to the woman, "See, your son is alive" (I Kings 17:23).

Elijah's disciple, Elisha, is also the divine instrument of bringing a youth back from death. Elisha prophesies that a barren Shunammite woman who had given him hospitality would bear a child. The prophecy is fulfilled and she bears a son, who subsequently dies. The distraught woman rushes to Elisha, who miraculously revives the child (2 Kings 4:34–37).

The death scenes of both Elijah and Elisha also portray images of resurrection. At the end of Elijah's earthly life's journey, the prophet ascends in a chariot of fire and is taken to heaven. The disciples of the prophet inform Elisha that his master Elijah will be "taken" away. The mantle of prophecy, along with the power of revival, is thereafter transferred to Elijah's disciple, Elisha.

A miraculous scene demonstrating Elisha's powers, even after his death, occurs when his body causes the revival of a dead man whose corpse is hastily thrown into the prophet's grave when a marauding band of Moabites appears. When the body of the dead man touches that of the prophet, "the (dead) man revived and stood on his feet" (2 Kings 13:20).

Nowhere else in the Hebrew Bible do we find narratives that deal so directly with the subject of resurrection. Miracle-working of this kind is not found again until the stories of the New Testament. Scholars are divided as to whether these are "true" resurrection narratives (for example, it may be argued that the children did not actually die, or were not buried, or that they were revived to live ordinary rather than everlasting lives).[7] What is clear from these stories is that Elijah and Elisha, in the context of proving that God had greater power than Baal, were capable of reversing the normal order of life and death. The idea of resurrection must have been extant among the people for these stories to have any force.

Verbs of Resurrection

According to Bible scholar John Sawyer, there are a small number of terms in a small number of passages that refer to the resurrection of the dead.[8]

In his view these passages are "clear expressions of God's power to create out of the dust and decay of the grave a new humanity where good lives do not end in suffering and justice prevails."[9]

The concept of resurrection, in his view, is alluded to by way of several specific verbs and expressions. It is important to note that the words themselves do not always connote resurrection, but that they do so when the context also suggests it. This means that the passages have to be read carefully in order to pick up on the linguistic usages and the allusions.

Most Hebrew verbs are based on three-letter roots that carry through all their conjugations. Sawyer makes the case that five of these roots form the core of resurrection language in the Hebrew Bible. These verbs are: "to wake up" (root *y-k-tz* or *k-y-tz*); "to stand up" (root *k-w-m*); "to live" (root *ḥ-y-h*); "to return" (root *sh-w-v*); and "to sprout forth" (root *tz-y-tz*) (although the last appears too infrequently to address in these pages). All of these verbs also appear elsewhere in the Hebrew Bible without connoting resurrection, but, for example, when "to stand up" appears paired and parallel with "to live," the combination strongly suggests that the resurrection motif is present. Leonard Greenspoon takes Sawyer's arguments a step further, suggesting that the presence of "to wake up" in the Daniel text, which is unambiguous in its reference to resurrection, means that it is the term that "best sums up what is characteristic of biblical resurrection."[10] To these five verbs, we will add a sixth, suggested by Mitchell Dahood: "to take" (root *l-k-ḥ*), whose appearance we already noted in the Elijah/Elisha stories.[11]

To Awaken

The basic meaning of the verb *yakatz,* indicated by the root *k-y-tz* or *y-k-tz* (cited by both Sawyer and Greenspoon in its causative form, *h-k-y-tz*) is "to wake up." If we examine the various occurrences of these two related roots across the Hebrew Bible, however, we find that more often than not they connote a change of state of some kind. Biblical Hebrew has a word for "ordinary" waking up, the root *'-w-r,* but when the root *k-y-tz* or *y-k-tz* is used, there is an additional degree of significance. For example, this is the verb used when Pharaoh wakes up suddenly from his mysterious dreams,[12] and when Elijah scornfully taunts the prophets of Baal that their God might be sleeping and should wake up.[13] Jacob wakes from his prophetic dream about the angels going up and down the ladder to heaven;[14] Noah wakes from his drunkenness;[15] Solomon wakes to find he has been dreaming[16] and when Gehazi, Elisha's servant, goes on ahead to lay the prophet's staff on the face of the dead boy, he reports "the boy did not awaken," with the clear meaning of "revive."[17] As we shall see in the following texts, this verb can and sometimes does connote a change of state that can be as extreme as that from death to life.

In one of his oracles against Babylon, the prophet Jeremiah condemns the wicked Babylonians to this endless sleep from which they will never awaken. The endless sleep mentioned in this passage can only be the sleep of death. Jeremiah is saying that the wicked deserve an eternity without the hope of resurrection. This punishment only makes sense when juxtaposed with the implied fate of the righteous, who are not doomed to an endless sleep, but who will one day "awaken" from their slumber.

> Babylon shall become rubble,
> A den for jackals,
> An object of horror and hissing,
> Without inhabitant.
> Like lions, they roar together,
> They growl like lion cubs.
> When they are heated, I will set out their drink
> And get them drunk that they may become giddy,
> And sleep an endless sleep, never to awaken,
> Declares the Lord.   (Jeremiah 51:37–39)

In distinguishing between the fates of the wicked and the righteous, this passage from Jeremiah affirms a belief in an afterlife in which God rewards righteousness and punishes wickedness.[18] Just as God causes endless sleep to some, the implication is that God is also able to revive the righteous after slumber (death) to eternal life.

If we now reconsider the passage from Daniel 12:2 with which we began our discussion, it becomes clear that the presence of the verb "to awaken" there borrows from antecedents where the term is linked to resurrection. Moreover, the verb "awaken" occurs there in combination with other verbs that connect to resurrection motifs, further reinforcing its significance as a "resurrection verb."

It has often been noted that there is an important intertexual link between the books of Daniel and Jeremiah. In Daniel 9:1–2, the post-exilic prophet Daniel reads and tries to interpret the seventy-year oracle of the pre-exilic prophet Jeremiah (Jeremiah 29:10) concerning the fate of Babylon and restoration of the Jews to Jerusalem:

> In the first year of his reign, I, Daniel, consulted the books
> concerning the number of years that, according to the
> word of the Lord that had come to Jeremiah the prophet,
> were to be the term of Jerusalem's desolation – seventy
> years. (Daniel 9:2)

The fact that Daniel was familiar with the literature of his predecessors lends further support to the idea that he may have been responsive to their ideas about resurrection and life after death.

To Take

The verb "to take" (*lakah*, root *l-k-h*) is used in the Bible both literally, for the taking of objects, and figuratively, as in the taking of a wife. In a small number of contexts, however, it is clear that the verb is being used to suggest being taken to a higher sphere or mode of existence.

There are two psalms in which the verb "to take" is utilized to express the pious person's hope for the reward of eternal life in God's presence. Both Psalms 49 and 73 (part of the genre known as "Wisdom Psalms") reflect on the theological problem of why it can happen that the wicked prosper and the righteous suffer, as well as the transitory nature of human life.

> But God will redeem my soul from the hand of Sheol, for
> He will take me. (Psalm 49:16)

Psalm 73 likewise speaks of the pious "being taken" to enjoy nearness to God's presence.[19]

> And I am constantly with You:
> You hold my right hand.
> You will lead me with your counsel
> And afterward take me with glory.   (Psalm 73:23–24)

The use of this verb in these psalms suggests that God will take the pious to everlasting life in heaven. The concluding message of these two psalms tells us that the just man who places his confidence in God rather than in material values of this world will be "taken" into the company of God and live forever. In the passage in Psalm 49, the syntax of the phrase is also consistent with the "death, then life" pattern observed earlier: first Sheol is mentioned, and then the resurrection verb.

The root for "to take" also appears together with the paired resurrection verbs "to live" and "to stand up" in the Elijah cycle. As we noted earlier, the verb is used to describe Elijah's ascension to heaven. Elisha has just requested a final gift: a double portion of his teacher's spirit. Elijah replies:

> You have asked a difficult thing . . . if you see me as I am
> being taken from you, this will be granted to you: if not,
> it will not.   (2 Kings 2:10)

Immediately afterwards, Elisha sees that Elijah is indeed "taken" to heaven on a fiery chariot.

The Hebrew Bible knows of only one other ascension besides Elijah, that of Enoch in Genesis 5:24, who was said to have walked with and had been taken by God. Clearly, the verb can be used with a mystical connotation. We should remember that it is commonly believed that the prophet Elijah never died, but that he ascended alive to heaven. In the prophetic book of Malachi, the last prophet of the Hebrew Bible (c. 450 B.C.E.), Elijah reappears and is referred to as the messenger who will come before the day of the Lord, which historically is taken to mean that he will herald the days of the Messiah (Malachi 3:23).

To Stand Up and To Live

As we saw in the Elijah narratives, the verb "to live," *ḥayah* (*ḥ-y-h*) is used to describe the children coming back to life. Elsewhere in the Bible, the verb "to live" is used in combination with the verb "to stand up/to get up," *'amad* (*'-m-d*) to create powerful images of resurrection, as we shall see in the prophecies of Ezekiel and Hosea.

Ezekiel lived through the greatest crises in ancient Israel's history: the ruin of its capital, Jerusalem, the destruction of the First Temple, the loss of Judah's independence, and the exile of its leading citizens to Babylon (597–586 B.C.E.). Each of these losses had historical, political and theological ramifications. Not only were the people's physical lives disrupted, but their faith was shaken as well. The suffering people cried out in their own defense, challenging the justness of the belief that the iniquities of the fathers are visited upon the children (Jeremiah 31:29; Ezekiel 18:4). Ezekiel agreed that the person alone should suffer for individual sins and not pay the price for the entire nation.

In his apocalyptic vision of the valley of the dry bones, the prophet responds to the people's despair and predicts national restoration. The imagery is powerful. The prophet speaks directly to the bones and delivers the word of God, predicting they will live again:

> O dry bones, hear the word of God.
> Thus says the Lord God to these bones,
> "Behold, I will cause breath to enter you, and you shall
> live again." (Ezekiel 37:4–5)

This imagery of resurrection is more than a metaphor for the revival of the collective body: it is a graphic depiction of physical resurrection.

> And I will lay sinews upon you and will bring up flesh
> upon you, and cover you with skin, and put breath in you,
> and you shall live; and you shall know that I am the Lord.
> (Ezekiel 37:6)

The key word "live," which appears five times in 37:1–14, alerts the reader to the theme of resurrection. Although we do not find the expected paired word "to rise," the synonym "to stand" does appear in verse 37:10:

> I prophesied as he commanded me. The breath entered
> them and they came to life and stood up on their feet, a
> vast multitude. (Ezekiel 37:10)

In the vision we find all the physical elements necessary for reconstructing the human body: bones, flesh, sinews, spirit, and the breath of life. This vision may symbolize the hope for national restoration but it is clearly a description of individual physical revival as well.[20]

Hosea prophesied in the northern kingdom of Israel in the mideighth century B.C.E. until the fall of its capital, Samaria, to the Assyrians in 721 B.C.E. His prophecies are set against a backdrop of social, moral, and religious decadence. The prophet castigates Israel for the syncretistic practice of worshipping God together with Baal and his Canaanite fertility cults.

Scholars once maintained that foreign influences emanating in particular from Babylonian, Persian and Canaanite-Ugaritic cultic beliefs influenced the Israelites' belief in the afterlife.[21] Current research, however, tends to conclude that foreign practices might not have had a decisive impact on the Israelites' specific understandings of resurrection. For example, the death and resurrection of the nature god Baal does not appear to explain the biblical concept of God's awakening mortals to new life after death. As one of the authors of the Anchor Bible commentaries writes, "the death and resurrection of people has nothing in common with a myth in which a god dies and comes back to life."[22] Although it may appear that there are similarities between the Canaanite rising and dying god myth and the Israelite belief in God's resurrection of people, they are actually unrelated. God is never described in the text as dying and rising. On the contrary, He is always the "Living God."

At the same time, Hosea may have known about the activities attributed to earlier prophets Elijah and Elisha concerning resurrection. Verses in Hosea feature several of the verbs previously indicated as signaling the resurrection motif, such as "to come back or turn back," "to live," and "to stand."

> Come, let us turn back to God:
> He has stricken, and He can heal us;
> He wounded, and He can bind us up.
> After two days He will revive us;
> On the third day He will raise us up,
> That we may live in His presence,
> And He shall come to us as rain,
> As the latter rain that waters the earth.　　(Hosea 6:1–3)

The first verse describes the people begging to be healed by God from their wounded state. The request in the second verse intensifies when the paired verbs "to live" and "to stand" appear, depicting the people asking not only to be healed but also to be revived.

By the end of the book of Hosea the resurrection theme is articulated more explicitly: "I will ransom them from the power of the grave (Sheol) and I will redeem them from death" (Hosea 13:14). At this juncture, we could say there are more hints of bodily resurrection than physical healing.

To Return

The idea of "returning" or "turning back" is denoted by the Hebrew verb *shuv* (root *sh-w-v*). It is typically used to signify repentance, as shown in the passage from Hosea 6: "Come, let us turn back to God." In several instances, it also seems to mean restoration and resurrection. For example, the appeal in the phrase "Restore us!" in this passage from the book of Psalms makes reference to resurrection through poetic allusion:

> O God of hosts, please turn again,
> Look down from heaven and see;
> Take note of that vine,

The stock planted by your right hand,
The stem you have adopted as your own.
For it is burned by fire and cut down,
Perishing before your angry blast.
Grant your help to the man at your right hand,
The one you have taken as your own.
We will not turn away from you;
Preserve our life that we may invoke your name.
O Lord, God of hosts, restore us to life;
Show your favor that we may be delivered.

(Psalm 80:15–20)

Although the psalmist may be beseeching God for help in the trials of this life, it is also possible that the author is hoping for something that exists beyond this world in the presence of God. It seems plausible that the poetic reference to the vine burned with fire alludes to untimely human death, so that the request for help and revival is a request for resurrection from death. Notable in the psalm above are the verbs used to refer to death and revival. The psalmist uses "to turn back" in the causative, in which mode it can mean "bring back," "rescue," or "restore."

When the passage speaks of the vine that met its demise by fire, the verbs used suggest an allusion to human death. In the second mention of the "stem" that is "adopted" by God (v. 16) the Hebrew word for "son" (*ben*) is used, but then, it is "burned by fire" and "cut down" (v. 17). Immediately the psalmist asks God to "restore us to life" and "deliver" us, indicating or alluding to a belief in divine intervention that allows life after death.

There are two passages in the Bible where the combined resurrection language – the density of subject matter and the verbs we have discussed – is especially strong. One is the text from Daniel 12:2, which we have already mentioned and will return to shortly; the other is the so-called "Isaiah Apocalypse," the prophet's teachings about the end of days, found in chapters 24–27 of the book of Isaiah.[23]

Biblical scholars have been divided on the dating of this part of the book of Isaiah but recent scholarship favors the sixth century B.C.E., around the time of the destruction of the First Temple. This century found the people of the southern kingdom of Judah faced with national destruction and dispersion by the Babylonians. The national trauma led many conquered Jews who were innocent of wrongdoing to question God's justice. Resurrection would then promise them vindication for their suffering and would reaffirm God's power in bringing the righteous back to life. If the sixth century B.C.E. were the date for the Isaiah Apocalypse, it would prove that belief in resurrection was already in evidence well before Daniel, as our discussion of Hosea, Ezekiel and Jeremiah has suggested.

Whereas the language of texts discussed earlier hints at a resurrection motif, this passage from Isaiah expresses an explicit description of belief in a hereafter. The text clearly asserts the resurrection of the dead, proclaiming that those who lie in the dust of the earth will rise and shout with joy:

> Oh, let Your dead revive!
> Let corpses arise!
> Awake and shout for joy,
> You who dwell in the dust!
> For Your dew is the dew on fresh growth;
> You make the land of the shades come to life.
>
> (Isaiah 26:19)

This passage has an especially high density of resurrection language: "revive," "arise," "awake." The strongest of the resurrection verbs, "to awaken," is used in combination with the two others, plus there is a reference to the *refa'im,* the ghosts or shades who inhabit Sheol. Here, *refa'im* refers not only to the wicked leaders who will not be revived after death but also the pious who will be healed, cast out of the netherworld and resurrected by the intervention of God.[24] In this way, *refa'im* serves as an all-encompassing term for the dead. Juxtaposed as it is with the other "resurrection" verbs, particularly "to live," the verse cannot be describing anything but a revival of the dead.[25]

Another striking motif of rebirth in this passage draws on imagery from nature. The image of dew reviving the dead is reminiscent of the vocabulary and language of nature worship from the surrounding cultures. However, in the Isaiah context, it is the life-giving power of God that resurrects the dead as the morning dew revives the flowers after a night of darkness. As dew brings life to the parched vegetation, so God will give new life through the dew as it falls on the graves of God's people. The idea that resurrection and water are connected on an imagistic level is a powerful one, as we saw in the reference to rain in the Hosea text: "And He shall come to us as rain, as the latter rain that waters the earth" (Hosea 6:3).

A corollary to this notion is Isaiah's wish that death will disappear forever:

> He will swallow death forever.
> And God will wipe away tears from all faces . . .
> For God has spoken.   (Isaiah 25:8)

Having discussed all of its antecedents, we can now return to Daniel 12:2, the passage with which we began our exploration:

> And many of those who sleep in the dust of the earth will
> awake, some to eternal life and some to reproaches and
> everlasting abhorrence. And the wise will be radiant like
> the bright expanse of sky, and those who lead the many to
> righteousness [will shine] like the stars forever and ever.
>   (Daniel 12:2–3)

Daniel's imagery of resurrection presents all the metaphors we have been discussing. His description of those who "sleep in the dust" is a clear reference to the dead, Sheol, the enigmatic underworld, and the grave. The verb "to live" appears paired with "to stand up," and the causative form of "to wake up" is there as well, emphasizing the resurrection theme. This passage is apparently the culmination of a long tradition of conceptualizing resurrection. What scholars previously understood as an idea suddenly bursting into bloom is actually a flowering from deeper roots, buried in the soil of earlier biblical writings.

As we have seen, throughout the Hebrew canon there are hints and allusions to an existence that continues beyond the grave. It is true that the belief is not set out in any straightforward way. It is also true that it is not the main focus of the Hebrew Bible, the majority of whose texts are devoted to other lofty ideas. Nonetheless, a fragile trail of evidence is there to follow. Poetry, narrative, vocabulary and syntax all conspire to convey the message. The passage in Daniel discussed above can now be seen in its proper context. Clearly, it sprang from the hints and allusions earlier in the Hebrew Bible, culminating in Daniel's fully developed imagery of a spiritual and physical resurrection.

The book of Daniel, consisting of twelve chapters, is set during the Babylonian exile, but as we mentioned earlier, there is some dispute about the dating of the book. Chapters 1–6 narrate a few stories about Daniel, the wise and pious person who is miraculously saved from the lions' den. In chapters 7–12, which includes Daniel's apocalyptic visions, the ostensible setting remains Babylonia as it passes to Persian rule; but in chapter 11, the author "foretells" the conquest of Persian territory by the Greeks and the persecution of Jews in the second century by Antiochus Epiphanes, culminating in the desecration of the Temple in 165 B.C.E.

If the later chapters of Daniel were written during the second century B.C.E., as some consider it to be (and as is suggested by the allusions to historical events in that century), it is clear that they would have been intended to offer hope and consolation to Jews suffering from oppression by the Syrian king, identified as Antiochus Epiphanes. This was a difficult time for pious Jews who, because they were observing God's law, were punished even to martyrdom. The injustice of this persecution may have led them to intensify their search for a belief that martyrs who died fighting for their religion would be rewarded by God with resurrection while their oppressors would be punished with abiding perdition.[26]

Traditional religious scholars date the book earlier, in the sixth century B.C.E.[27] If that is the case, the presence of the resurrection theme in the book is explained by the fact that resurrection was a subject that was present in the cultural milieu of the time. As we saw in Ezekiel and Jeremiah, the people balked at being punished for the sins of their parents. The proposition in the Daniel passage – that some people will be granted eternal life and others condemned to eternal damnation – might be a proposed answer to this quandary, asserting that there is individual provision in the afterlife, depending on one's actions in this one.

While both Isaiah and Daniel portray scenarios in which the dead are returned to life, Isaiah views resurrection as a reward only for the righteous, whom he cites specifically as those who will "arise and sing." In contrast, Daniel proclaims that both the righteous and their persecutors will be resurrected. However, Daniel's vision distinguishes between the fates of those who are returned to life: the righteous will *arise* for eternal life, while the others, namely the persecutors of the righteous, will *awaken* to shame and punishment.

We see, then, that the book of Daniel did not come out of nowhere to introduce the concept of resurrection in the Hebrew Bible, but incorporates familiar themes and images of resurrection from earlier biblical texts. On the one hand, the book of Daniel draws together the glimmerings of ancient Israel's belief in the hereafter; on the other hand, this book represents a starting point, because it marks the beginning of a tangible ideology of the afterlife. Daniel becomes the jumping-off place for post-biblical belief in bodily resurrection in rabbinic Judaism (and the Sadducees' rejection of the same concept), as well as the divergent interpretation adopted by early Christianity in the Second Temple period.

Early Post-Biblical Literature: Gateways to Heaven and Hell

I F THE HEBREW Bible is relatively reticent on the subject of an afterlife, we encounter a large body of literature in the post-biblical period filled with speculations about what follows death. This collection of books, known by its Greek names as the Apocrypha (meaning "hidden") and Pseudepigrapha (meaning "falsely ascribed to a particular author"), was written by a group of unknown authors living both inside and outside the land of Israel from approximately 200 B.C.E. to 200 C.E. The texts in the Apocrypha and the Pseudepigrapha represent the only significant Jewish literature bridging the gap between the Hebrew Bible and the earliest writings of the rabbis.

There is some dispute among scholars as to the exact number of books in the Apocrypha because different scholars divide the books in various ways. Published versions generally list between eleven and fifteen separate books. They include some that we will discuss for their views on the afterlife, such as Esdras, Maccabees, Ben Sira and the Wisdom of Solomon, and other writings that have passed into Jewish legend, such as the story of Judith. These books are replete with historical, legendary, prophetic, and moralistic ethical writings, offering a rich source of material about Jewish life in the Second Temple period.

The Pseudepigrapha are comprised predominantly of apocalyptic writings, prophecies predictive of the "end of days," an end-time to human history as we know it.[1] The apocalyptic imagery of the Pseudepigrapha, contained in texts such as the Book of Jubilees, 1 Enoch, 4 Maccabees, 4 Ezra, and 2 Baruch, is drawn from some of the Hebrew prophets, but its most important source is the book of Daniel, chapters 7–12. There we read about Daniel's visions of fabulous beasts rising from the sea, a mysterious man coming in with the clouds of heaven, and another older man, the "Ancient of Days," appearing on a throne of fiery flames. Angels come to Daniel to interpret his mystical visions.

Building on these scenarios, the Pseudepigrapha contain revelations written by anonymous authors that are ascribed to biblical characters such as Enoch, Abraham, Elijah, Moses, and Ezra. They claim to provide hidden information about the fate of humanity as well as divine instructions concerning the end of days.

WHY ARE THESE BOOKS NOT IN THE HEBREW BIBLE?

The first question we need to ask is why these books were not preserved as part of the Jewish scriptures. Were they considered for the biblical canon, and if so, why were they not included?

The story of the canonization of the Hebrew Bible is complex and took place in stages that extended over hundreds of years. The term "canon," a Greek borrowing, is derived from the Hebrew word *kaneh*, a cutting of cane reed used as a measuring instrument. The term came to be used in a metaphorical sense, indicating a standard measurement to establish the ethical and religious content of a particular collection of writings and to decide which were deemed worthy of being included in the Bible. There was no real dispute about including the Five Books of Moses and the Prophets.[2] As for the Writings (*Ketuvim*), the Mishnah offers anecdotal evidence that the question of whether to include certain books was still being hotly debated by the rabbis at Yavneh around 90 C.E. The sages are described as meeting at length to decide whether the Song of Songs and Ecclesiastes should be included in the canon.[3]

No such dispute, however, is recorded for the apocryphal literature.

The rabbis, as we will see, considered these to be "outside books" that did not qualify for the honor of being included in the canon. While the Apocrypha were not included in the Hebrew Bible, they were eventually accepted into the Septuagint, the Greek translation of the Hebrew Bible, which was not widely used by Jews, but was read by early Christians.

There is also an important difference between the apocryphal and pseudepigraphical writings. The apocryphal books, as we mentioned, were included in the Septuagint and later given secondary or "deutero-canonical" status in the Catholic (but not the Protestant) Bible. The Pseudepigrapha, however, never achieved *any* canonical status in either Jewish or Christian tradition. Nonetheless, the entire body of post-biblical literature, both the Apocrypha and the Pseudepigrapha, eventually gained great popularity in Christian circles, and thus the books survive to the present day.

The rabbis of the talmudic era largely either ignored or disparaged these writings as unworthy of study, let alone inclusion in the canon. In Mishnah *Sanhedrin* 10:1 it is stated, "All Israel have a share in the World to Come." Thereupon follow numerous exceptions to this rule, such as "one who claims the Torah is not from heaven." Another exception is given in the name of Rabbi Akiva: "He who reads *sefarim hitzoni'im* [external books], has no share in the World to Come."

In their discussion of Mishnah *Sanhedrin* 10:1, the rabbis of the Babylonian Talmud arrive at the conclusion that these "external" books are the books of the *minim*, members of heretical sects. Still some Babylonian rabbis agreed with the prevailing Palestinian view that while the non-canonical books were not holy enough to be read publicly, neither were they heretical, and they could be read for private study.[4] They warned, however, that one should not meditate or ponder over them as one would when studying Torah.[5]

In the Palestinian Talmud, Rabbi Akiva seems to be following a more lenient approach to the non-canonical writings:

> Rabbi Akiva says, "He who reads external books such as Ben Sira, or Ben Laanah, the books of Homeros and all books which were written from that time onwards,

he who reads them is as he who reads an *iggeret* [secular document]."[6]

The term *iggeret* might suggest a form of reading material meant not for the type of intense religious study that assured one's place in the World to Come, but for reading at home.

Ben Sira, a sage and scribe of the second century B.C.E., is the only author of an apocryphal text mentioned by name or quoted in rabbinic literature. The rabbis may have had a somewhat positive regard for the book of Ecclesiasticus (Ben Sira), since they occasionally quote his maxims. For instance, a maxim attributed to Rabbi Levitas of Yavneh reads: "Be exceedingly lowly of spirit, for the hope of man is but the worm (*Pirke Avot* 4:4)." But the words of "Rabbi Levitas" appear to be a direct quotation from Ecclesiasticus (Ben Sira) 7:17: "Humble altogether all your pride, for man's expectation is worms."

There are other references to Ben Sira in the Talmud, some negative, and others acknowledging his wisdom.[7] For example, in the Babylonian Talmud (*Sanhedrin* 100b), the statement by one rabbi that it is forbidden to read Ben Sira is followed by a discussion in which several colleagues argue for the value of the writings. This discussion, as well as quotations of Ben Sira in the Talmud, suggest that some of the rabbis regarded Ben Sira's teachings, which ranged widely over the spiritual and worldly topics, as being worthy of the canon and were probably excluded because of the Greek-influenced secular ideas that he expressed.[8]

In an audacious move, the pseudepigraphic book of Esdras IV (the Greek name for Ezra) claims canonical status for itself – as well as divine origin for all the apocryphal and pseudepigraphical books:

> As for me [Ezra], I spoke in the daytime and was not silent at night. So during the forty days ninety-four books were written. And when the forty days were ended, the Most High spoke to me, saying, "Make public the twenty-four books that you wrote first and let the worthy and the unworthy read them; but keep the seventy that were written last, in order to give them to the wise among your

people. For in them is the spring of understanding, the
fountain of wisdom, and the river of knowledge.[9]

Here the twenty-four books might be the books of the Hebrew Bible,
while the seventy books written last most likely refer to the Apocrypha
and Pseudepigrapha. 2 Esdras suggests that there was a tradition of
esoteric learning in the apocryphal literature that the author traces back
to Abraham and Moses. The pseudepigraphic "Ezra" reveals that he is
commanded to teach and give this learning to "the wise among [his]
people" (2 Esdras 12:37 and 14:46). These writings, as we will see, played
an important role in promoting belief in resurrection and immortality.

Most of these books were originally written in Hebrew or Aramaic
except for the Wisdom of Solomon, 2 Maccabees, and a few others,
which were originally written in Greek.[10] Today we have only the Greek
versions, the one exception being the Wisdom of Ben Sira (Ecclesiasticus), which does exist in a Hebrew version.[11] Despite their non-inclusion
in the Hebrew canon, these books were still influential. For example, 1
Maccabees is primarily a historical account of the Maccabean revolt and
subsequent wars between 175–135 B.C.E. These dramatic events led to
the Maccabeans' recapturing of Jerusalem and the rededication of the
Temple in 165 B.C.E. In 1 Maccabees 4:59, we read the text that establishes the post-biblical festival of Hanukkah: "Judah and his brethren . . .
ordained that the days of the dedication should be kept in their season
from year to year for eight days from the twenty-fifth of Kislev, with glad-
ness and joy." The apocryphal text does not include the miracle of the
one day's supply of oil lasting for eight, which was a story narrated by the
rabbis in the Babylonian Talmud to play down the militaristic aspects of
Hanukkah and place it on a more spiritual plane (BT *Shabbat* 21b).

There are numerous examples of apocryphal works with a lasting impact on Jewish culture. The book of Judith contains the story,
linked to Hanukkah by tradition and told to this day, of a pious Judean
widow who tricked the general of the enemy's army into drinking too
much wine and decapitated him in his sleep. Likewise, The Wisdom
of Ben Sira includes the basis for several well-known Hebrew blessings, such as the blessing upon seeing a rainbow, and the first known

reference to the *Shemoneh Esrei,* the central prayer of the Jewish service.[12]

The Apocrypha and Pseudepigrapha also reflect a range of theological reactions to the tumultuous events of the Second Temple period, beginning with the rebellion against Syrian-Greek oppression and ending with two crushed rebellions against Roman tyranny. They also contain significantly expanded views of the afterlife, including such topics as bodily resurrection, the immortality of the soul, reward and punishment, and divine judgment.

ॐ   RESURRECTION AND IMMORTALITY

The post-biblical texts of the Apocrypha and Pseudepigrapha open a window onto Second Temple thinking about death and afterlife, which began to include influences from cultures in which Jews of the period lived. One such influence, imported from the Greeks, was the addition of a concept of the immortality of the soul to the already-established belief in bodily resurrection. Some of the texts below cite a belief in resurrection (as a reward for righteousness), while others favor the soul's immortality.

Apocrypha: 2 Maccabees

Written in Greek by an anonymous author, 2 Maccabees covers the turbulent events of the years 175–160 B.C.E., when the Jews were fighting for their independence from the Greeks. The author describes the book as being a summary of five books by one Jason of Cyrene, a Jewish historian of the second century B.C.E. who wrote an account of the Maccabean revolt. Its style is quite rhetorical and the story is told in a very dramatic way.[13]

In the seventh chapter of the book, we find the tragic story of a mother and her seven sons who die as martyrs when they refuse to worship the idols of the oppressor, Antiochus Epiphanes, who tried to mandate Hellenistic cult practices in Jerusalem. The seven boys are tortured in the presence of their mother in the most cruel manner. One after the other, they proclaim their readiness to die for God because of their unshakeable belief in resurrection. Rather than desecrating the Torah, eating pork, or bowing down to an idol, they declare their belief that "the King of the Universe will resurrect us, who die for the sake of his laws, to a new eternal life."[14] The martyrs are confident that the reward for their sacrifice in the hereafter will be resurrection. One son, at the point of death from torture, says:

> Better it is to pass away from among men while looking forward in hope to the fulfillment of God's promises that we shall be resurrected by Him, for you shall have no resurrection unto life.[15]

The mother[16] demonstrates remarkable resolve as she encourages the sons to give up their young lives for God. She even urges the youngest boy not to submit to the king's demand for apostasy, saying:

> It is the Creator of the Universe who molds man at his birth and plans the origin of all things. Therefore He, in his mercy, will give you back life and breath again, since now you put His laws above all thought of self.[17]

Her words imply a faith in the redemptive power of martyrdom and the ultimate reunification of the family in another world. The language is explicit, using the Greek term, *anastasis,* for resurrection.

The story of the mother and her seven sons has resonated with the Jewish people for centuries and was considered important enough, some six hundred years after it was written, to include in the Talmud. It is cited in the context of a long discussion of incidents of martyrdom that occurred at the time of the destruction of the Second Temple.[18]

The preceding chapter of 2 Maccabees describes another martyr who shows great courage. He is an elderly scribe named Eleazar who also defies the tyrant Antiochus. He refuses even to pretend to eat forbidden food in order to save his own life, but chooses rather to be a role model for the young people observing him so that they will remain steadfast in their faith. While he makes no explicit reference to resurrection, there is a hint of it in his dying words:

> The Lord, who possesses sacred knowledge, perceives that, though I could have escaped death, in my body I submit to cruel torment under the lash, and He knows that in my soul I am glad to suffer it out of reverence for Him.[19]

Later, when we look at the pseudepigraphal book 4 Maccabees, we will see that the author retells the same story of Eleazar's martyrdom but describes his faith in terms of a belief in the soul's immortality.

Apocrypha: The Wisdom of Solomon

Dating from approximately the first century B.C.E., the Wisdom of Solomon is a combination of Greek philosophy and Jewish theology and may well be the first Jewish source that explicitly depicts personal immortality as a reward for righteousness. The book is presented as a continuation of the genre known as Wisdom Literature, which includes the biblical books of Proverbs, Job and Ecclesiastes.

The Wisdom of Solomon was probably written by a Greek Jew in Alexandria after the city's conquest by Rome in 30 B.C.E. The writer assumes the identity of King Solomon, who speaks in praise of wisdom and righteousness and warns against the sins of oppression, idolatry, and rampant materialism. Not only is the writer willing to accept the imported Greek belief in immortality of the soul, but he also displays readiness to revise some of the traditional beliefs of his Jewish faith. Thus, he never mentions the concept of bodily resurrection (*anastasis*), preferring instead to discuss immortality (*aqansia*). The Wisdom of Solomon contains other ideas that diverge from traditional Jewish and biblical views as well; for example, he denies that suffering presupposes sin or that barrenness is a mark of divine displeasure.[20] Moreover, he does not regard earthly death as a calamity.

The great contrast between the punishment of the wicked and the reward of the righteous is a recurring theme in the Wisdom of Solomon. In this context, the author continually stresses faith in the immortality of the soul:

> For God created man for immortality
> And made him the image of His own eternity . . . .[21]

The wicked, according to the author, believe that life is chance and death is final and therefore one should enjoy the pleasures of this life without regard to moral scruples. But, the author argues, the wicked are so blinded by their own iniquity that they are ignorant of God's mysteries and forsake the prize of immortality. While the wicked may seem to prosper in this life, they are not aware that they face judgment by God in the future:

> And [the wicked] had no virtue to show,
> But were consumed in wickedness,
> For the ungodly man's hope is like chaff carried by the
>   wind . . . .
> But the upright live forever,
> And their reward is with the Lord,
> And the Most High takes care of them.
> Therefore they will receive the glorious kingdom. . . .[22]

The author's attitude is not entirely Greek, however. The Greeks believed in the immortal nature of *all* souls. In the Wisdom of Solomon, it is clear that immortality is dependent on the practice of justice. By their good behavior, the righteous are made immortal. This is a rabbinic twist on the Greek concept, following the same path pursued by Philo, the Jewish philosopher who lived in Alexandria in the first century. Influenced not only by Greek philosophy but by biblical tradition as well, Philo implies that only the souls of the wise enjoy immortality.[23] This assertion continues to be reflected in rabbinic thinking about the path of righteousness leading to *ha-olam ha-ba*, the World to Come.[24]

Pseudepigrapha: The Book of Jubilees

Written in Hebrew between 135 B.C.E. and 105 B.C.E., but extant only in Ethiopic, the book of Jubilees consists of a rewriting of the events from creation to the revelation of the Law at Sinai. The anonymous author, who presents himself as an angel of the "Divine Presence," offers a sectarian, pietistic view of Jewish law and theology that departs in some ways from the developing normative Judaism of the day in Jerusalem. The author's purpose was to rewrite Jewish history from the beginning to emphasize the sect's ideas about Jewish law and practice and to remind Israel of its unique role.

Although the book is primarily devoted to a rewriting and expansion of biblical history, it does once deal with the life hereafter. The passage occurs at the end of an apocalyptic prediction of the woes to be suffered by later generations. Famine, war, and punishment are succeeded by a renewed commitment to commandments and righteousness, with people living up to a thousand years as a result of this good behavior. They will then die, the author says, but their spirits will continue to experience joy:

> And at that time the Lord will heal his servants
> And they will rise up and see great peace
> And drive out their adversaries.
> And the righteous shall see and be thankful
> And rejoice with joy forever and ever
> And shall see all their judgments and all their curses on
>   their enemies.
> And their bones shall rest in the earth
> And their spirits shall have much joy,
> And they shall know that it is the Lord who executes
>   judgment
> And shows mercy to hundreds and thousands and to all
>   that love Him.[25]

It is notable that this author seems to reject the idea of bodily resurrection ("their bones will rest in the earth"), opting instead for the idea that the soul will be immortal. Here we see an echo of the tension we noted in the apocryphal literature above. The discussion of whether there will be bodily resurrection or immortality of the soul will continue to mark the pseudepigraphic literature, opening a dialogue that takes place, as we shall see, over hundreds of years of Jewish history.

Pseudepigrapha: 4 Maccabees

The pseudepigraphic work of 4 Maccabees returns to the subject of the Hasmonean revolt, but this time deliberately emphasizing the theme of immortality over resurrection. Probably written in the first century C.E., the text is in the form of a philosophical discourse. The martyrdoms of Eleazar and the mother and her seven sons in 2 Maccabees are revisited, again with very detailed descriptions both of the tortures the martyrs were forced to undergo and the words they said. But here the author's knowledge of Greek philosophy seems to have influenced his description of events because the references to resurrection found in 2 Maccabees are transformed into references to immortality:

> Not one of the seven lads turned coward, but all, as though running on the highway to immortality, hurried on to death by torture.[26]

The author also mentions that Eleazar achieved immortality, even though he himself made no reference to life after death:

> The price for victory was incorruption in long-lasting life. The first to enter the contest was Eleazar, but the mother of the seven sons competed also, and the brothers as well took part.[27]

The book ends with a description of the martyrs' reward: "pure and deathless souls":

> But the sons of Abraham, together with their mother, who won the victor's prize, are gathered together in the choir

of their fathers, having received pure and deathless souls from God, to whom be glory forever and ever. Amen.[28]

✺   HEAVEN, HELL, AND JUDGMENT DAY

Apocalyptic literature, of which the book of Enoch is a prime example, is replete with allusions to heaven and hell, some of them descriptive as well as metaphorical. The authors of apocalyptic writings are generally personages using the names of biblical characters who are taken on journeys in which they see the upper and nether worlds, the living and the dead, the righteous and the wicked. "Enoch" is taken on such an extensive cosmic tour where he learns secrets shared only with the "elect," encounters demons and angels, and sees the realms of heaven and hell where souls await the Day of Judgment.

Pseudepigrapha: 1 Enoch

The Book of Enoch is probably the most intriguing book of the whole body of Apocrypha and Pseudepigrapha on the subject of the hereafter because it deals not only with the fate of the individual soul but with the fate of humankind. As a work of eschatology, it ties together the notions of the soul's journey after death with an end-point in time, a Day of Judgment, and a spiritual Messiah who presides over human destiny.

The source for the myth of Enoch, the man who journeys through the heavens and describes the heavenly precincts, is one enigmatic verse from the book of Genesis:

> Enoch walked with God, and he was no more, for God took him.

This verse is generally understood to mean that Enoch never died, but ascended to heaven alive. Interpretation and speculation about this figure, which began early, endeavored to explain where he was and what his visions could teach us. Stories were woven around Enoch that attributed knowledge of the secret mysteries of the world, including heavenly bodies and the calculation of time through the solar calendar, the cosmic disorder of the days of judgment, and the future unfolding of human history. Enoch comes to represent the most characteristic figure in apocalyptic literature.

There are three books of Enoch: (a) 1 Enoch is in Ethiopic, although fragments of the work also exist in Aramaic, Greek and Latin. It was written, scholars believe, between the second century B.C.E. and the first century C.E. (b) 2 Enoch, date unknown, is known only from manuscripts in Old Slavonic, which contain several gaps, and deals with the events of Enoch's life up to the onset of the flood. (c) 3 Enoch, which is attributed to Rabbi Ishmael, is an account of how Enoch journeyed into heaven. The angel Metatron, whom Rabbi Ishmael meets in heaven, declares – "I am Enoch the son of Jared" – which is how the book acquired its name. It is written in Hebrew and dates from the fifth to sixth century C.E.

The only book in the corpus that we shall discuss, 1 Enoch, is of unknown authorship and shares many characteristics with other pseudepigraphic works. Some scholars attribute it to a Palestinian Jew, others to a Jew living in Egypt. It poses the problem of theodicy, questioning how, if there is a just God, there can be so much suffering in the world. To answer this question, it offers ideas concerning reward in heaven and punishment in hell, about a time of judgment, about the coming of a spiritual messiah – as opposed to a royal redeemer or human king – to relieve oppression.

In the first part of the book, Enoch proclaims that God will bless the righteous elect and destroy the wicked on the Day of Judgment (chapters 1–5). The presence of evil in the world is attributed to the immoral actions of fallen angels who had intercourse with earthly women and caused a kind of mixed breed, half angel, half human, called the *nephilim*, to be born into the world, as described in Genesis 6. A group of fallen angels ask Enoch to intercede for them before his journey.

After this introduction Enoch is taken on a lengthy tour of the underworld, Sheol, then up to the heavenly bodies. On this journey he sees visions of the celestial counterparts of the Tree of Life, Jerusalem, and the Garden of Eden. The author also records detailed descriptions of a realm that seems very much like hell – a place where the wicked suffer incredible torment.

In his vision, Enoch meets with the angel Raphael and plies him with questions about all that he sees. At one point, Enoch is standing in the "place of punishment of fallen stars." Raphael explains how the sinners will be judged on the remote Day of Judgment, when they will be separated from the souls of the just:

> And he [Raphael] replied and said to me: "These three [areas] have been made in order that the spirits of the dead might be separated. And in the manner in which the souls of the righteous are separated by this spring of water with light upon it, in like manner the sinners are set apart when they die and are buried in the earth and judgment has not been executed on them in their lifetime . . . ."[29]

This passage indicates that sinners will remain earthbound, denied resurrection, with their souls in torment, while the immortal souls of the righteous rise to heaven. The idea of the righteous arising, but not the wicked, is similar to what we encountered in Daniel 12:2. A third area, described in subsequent verses, is a sort of limbo where souls neither suffer nor attain resurrection.

These themes of judgment are mentioned repeatedly in the book of Enoch and linked specifically to the promise of resurrection on a future day of reckoning:

> And he shall choose the righteous and the holy ones from among them [the dead ones], for the day when they shall be selected and saved has arrived. In those days the elect shall sit on my throne . . . .[30]

Another passage describes resurrection as arising from sleep:

> Then the righteous shall arise from his sleep, and the wise one shall arise and he shall be given unto them [the

people], and through him the roots of oppression shall be cut off.[31]

1 Enoch also presents a clear and detailed vision of the Messiah, which it calls "the Elect One." It is one of the first known Jewish sources to describe the Messiah as an ageless being inspired by God who, on the Day of Judgment, will judge all mortal beings:

> This is the Son of Man to whom belongs righteousness and with whom righteousness dwells. And he will open up all the hidden storerooms, for the Lord of the spirits has chosen him, and he is destined to be victorious before the Lord of the spirits in eternal uprightness. This one will remove the kings and the mighty ones from their comfortable seats and the strong ones from their thrones. The faces of the strong shall be slapped and filled with shame and gloom.[32]

This messiah differs from the one we read about in the Hebrew Bible, who was a leader anointed by God, an earthly king charged with leading and defending the people. Unlike Enoch's supernatural being, the biblical Messiah is a human of flesh and blood, though of the highest spiritual qualities, as depicted in the book of Isaiah:

> The spirit of the Lord shall alight upon him:
> A spirit of wisdom and insight,
> A spirit of counsel and valor,
> A spirit of devotion and reverence for the Lord.
>
> (Isaiah 11:2)

By contrast, the Messiah in 1 Enoch and other pseudepigraphical writings is unambiguously an eschatological figure: a transcendent being who will preside over the judgment of souls and the resurrection of the righteous at the end of days and will act as a leader of the righteous in the next world. The apocalyptic tone of these post-biblical writings about the Messiah, resurrection, and judgment resurface in the Christian book of Revelations, with its emphasis on end-times and its otherworldly imagery.

Pseudepigrapha: 4 Ezra

As the Palestinian Jews endured the punishing rule of the Romans after the destruction of the Second Temple, some sages tried to respond with texts that explained why the innocent suffer and promised a day of reckoning that would bring justice for the individual. It was in this milieu that 4 Ezra was composed in about 100 C.E., probably in Palestine. The author directs his vision of the afterlife to a community of Jews who had suffered greatly and hoped for future salvation, linking the future of the group to the fate of each individual.

The name "Ezra" (also known in this book as Salathiel) is a reference to Ezra the Scribe, the leader described in the biblical book of Ezra and a highly esteemed figure in rabbinic literature. The Talmud states concerning Ezra: "When the Torah was forgotten from Israel, Ezra came up from Babylon and reestablished it" (BT *Sukkot* 20a). Ezra thus is recognized as having a profound influence on building up Jewish life and Judaism when the Jews returned to the land of Judea after the Babylonian exile. The writer of the pseudepigraphical book 4 Ezra, aware of his importance, probably decided to name the document after him in order to invest the work with credibility and authority.

This book deals with the enigma of God's treatment of His people. Ezra asks why God's people are enslaved and suffering while the heathen prosper and rejoice. How, he asks, can God punish Israel using nations like Babylon, whose people are not faithful to God in keeping his law? The angel Uriel provides the answer in a series of dream visions similar to those in the book of Daniel. Uriel tells Ezra that God is the infinite Creator whose ways are far above those of humanity; accordingly, no human can understand God perfectly or, therefore, follow God's law perfectly. Yet God loves Israel now and forever.[33]

Chapter 7 of 4 Ezra contains the core of the book's teachings on the afterlife:

> For behold, the time will come, when the signs which I
> have foretold to you will come to pass . . . . And the earth
> shall give up those who are asleep in it, and the chambers
> will give up the souls that have been committed to them.
> And the Most High will be revealed upon the seat of
> judgment, and compassion shall pass away, and patience
> shall be withdrawn; but judgment alone shall remain,
> truth shall stand, and faithfulness shall grow strong.[34]

Following this passage is the most graphic and complete description of post-mortem existence in all apocryphal literature, showing the reward of the pious taken to paradise and the punishment of the wicked doomed to the furnace of hell: "Such spirits shall not enter into habitations, but shall immediately wander about on torments, ever grieving and sad, in seven ways."[35]

Significantly, 4 Ezra proceeds to introduce us to an idea that will find greater prominence later in Jewish tradition: the notion that there are varying levels of heaven and hell. After death, one is assigned to one of the seven levels of heaven or one of the seven realms of torment, based on his or her conduct on earth.[36] Thus, the author of 4 Ezra envisions an afterlife that has a number of phases in it. The ultimate resolution of a person's fate seems to be postponed to an indefinite future time.

But what happens to the soul immediately after the death of the physical body? In a conversation with an accompanying angel, Ezra asks this question directly:

> After death, as soon as we yield up our souls, shall we be
> kept in rest until you renew the creation, or shall we be
> tormented at once?[37]

The angel evades a direct answer, while reassuring Ezra that his good behavior would be rewarded at the end of days:

> I will show you that also, but do not be associated with
> those who have shown scorn, nor number yourself

among those who are tormented. For you have a treasure
of works laid up with the Most High; but it will not be
shown to you until the last times.[38]

Postmortem existence in 4 Ezra represents the integration of individual and collective eschatology. Taken as a whole, the book ties the fate
of the entire nation with the fate of the individual. This tension between
the collective and individual destiny will continue in later Jewish literature about the afterlife.

Pseudepigrapha: 2 Baruch

This book, also known as the Syriac Apocalypse of Baruch, is notable for
its extensive treatment of the subject of resurrection. It is of composite
authorship, and scholars date it at approximately the first or second
decade of the second century C.E. It was written in Palestine, originally in
Hebrew, before being translated into Syriac. Scholars view it as a critical
book for understanding how Jews of that period addressed the trauma
of the destruction of the Temple and the subsequent dispersion. The
author of the book appears to be an expert on both apocalyptic imagery
and rabbinic law, someone who could find a way to continue studying the
Law after the catastrophe of national destruction in 70 C.E., and therefore
someone who could help the Jewish people face the challenges of the
post-Temple era.[39]

Although the book was most likely written after the destruction of
the Second Temple, its narrative is set after the destruction of the First
Temple in 586 B.C.E. It consists of lamentations, prayers, and questions posed by Baruch to God, answers to those questions, and various
apocalyptic passages. It concludes with a letter addressed to Jews in the
dispersion in which Baruch urges them to trust in God and obey God's
commandments.

The initial part of the book deals with why it is important to live
righteously. Baruch then fasts for seven days before announcing twelve
disasters, which will be followed by the coming of the Messiah, the resurrection of the dead, and the final judgment:

> And it will happen after these things when the time of the
> appearance of the Anointed One has been fulfilled and
> he returns with glory, that then all who sleep in hope of
> him will rise. And it will happen at that time that those
> treasuries will be opened in which the souls of the right-
> eous were kept, and they will go out and the multitudes
> of the souls will appear together, in one assemblage, of
> one mind. And the first ones will enjoy themselves and
> the last ones will not be sad . . . .[40]

Later in the book, Baruch asks how those who are resurrected will
appear. God answers Baruch that they will be returned in their earthly
form:

> For the earth will surely give back the dead at that time:
> it receives them now in order to keep them, not changing
> anything in their form. But as it has received them, so it
> will give them back. And as I have delivered them to it so
> it will raise them. For then it will be necessary to show
> those who live that the dead are living again, and that
> those who went away have come back . . . .[41]

The subsequent chapter (51) however goes on to explain that after
the Day of Judgment, the bodies of those who were righteous will be
changed into "the splendor of angels," while those who were evil will be
changed into "startling visions and horrible shapes." Those who hoped in
the Law will be rewarded, and this reward is described in ecstatic detail,
concluding with the statement that "the excellence of the righteous will
then be greater than that of the angels."[42]

Once again we see here the theme of the righteous and the wicked
having separate destinies, a theme given prominence in the book of Daniel. We also see an emphasis on the necessity for righteous behavior. It is
notable that this author opts for resurrection, rather than immortality, as
defining the life hereafter. As we shall see when we consider mainstream
rabbinic thought, this is the idea that finally took hold and became a
cornerstone of rabbinic and post-rabbinic Judaism.

Along with the texts described above, several other passages within the Pseudepigrapha explicitly mention resurrection of the dead in a biblical sense. The Testaments of the Twelve Patriarchs present a kind of "ethical will" from each of Jacob's sons, in which each biblical character states his beliefs for the benefit of future generations. Of those, the Testament of Benjamin, which states "Enoch, Seth, Abraham, Isaac, and Jacob shall be raised up ... [A]ll men shall rise, some unto glory and some unto shame" (10:6–8), and the Testament of Judah, which asserts that "Abraham, Isaac, and Jacob will be resurrected unto life .... And those who die in sorrow shall be raised in joy" (25:1, 4) make explicit reference to physical resurrection.[43] Other sections of the patriarchal testaments refer to resurrection obliquely, and one, the Testament of Asher, suggests a belief in immortality of the soul, calling it "eternal life."[44]

Finally, the Sibylline Oracles, writings from the second century B.C.E. that borrow a pagan format of prophecy to express Jewish hopes for what will happen at the end of days,[45] make specific reference to resurrection:

> God himself will again form the bones and ashes of men,
> And he will raise up mortals again, as they were before....
> [A]s many as are godly will live again on earth,
> when God gives breath and life and grace to them ....[46]

Resurrection is seen as a creative act of God, an echo of God's first creation of man in Genesis 1.[47]

As we have seen, the Apocrypha and the Pseudepigrapha literature are a rich source of material about the afterlife. Their explicit references to bodily resurrection and immortality of the soul stand in stark contrast to the Hebrew Bible, with its veiled hints and allusions. Although they were considered "outside books" by the rabbis, these were Jewish books by Jewish authors that were read by their contemporaries. Why were speculations about the hereafter of such great interest at this time?

One theory is that the books provided comfort for people who were suffering. The historical context of the books bears this out: for example, 2 Maccabees was written when people were feeling humiliated and cast down by Greek tyranny, and 4 Ezra must be understood against the backdrop of Roman domination of the Jewish people in the first century that led up to the destruction of the Jerusalem Temple in 70 C.E. Similarly, 1 Enoch was written at a time of historical turmoil and human suffering that may have been perceived as unjust and undeserved. Apocalyptic writing is typical at a time of turmoil; some people are comforted by the idea that this world will end and what comes next will be better.

Underlying this simple historical argument, though, is a more complex idea. The problem of why the wicked prosper and the good suffer is one with which philosophers of every generation have wrestled. The concept of an afterlife provides one answer to the problem of evil. An afterlife provides reassurance that the suffering we endure in this existence is not worthless; instead, it is part of a greater pattern. The concept of the afterlife in Jewish thought will be expanded over time into a wider framework that will grow to include themes of judgment, accountability, punishment, and vindication. Even though the Apocrypha and the Pseudepigrapha were never accepted into the canon, they formed an undercurrent that fed Jewish thought about life after death when the subject was much on Jewish minds. They undoubtedly had a much greater influence on early Christian doctrine, which may be one reason that they are downplayed by later Jewish scholars. Many of the themes we first see laid out in this literature – final judgment, the fate of the wicked, the realms in which life after death is conducted – become paramount in Christian ideology, but they continue to appear, as we shall see, in rabbinic texts about the afterlife as well.

3

The Mishnah: Who Will Merit the World to Come?

ALL ISRAELITES HAVE a portion in the World to Come," according to the Mishnah, "but these people have no share in the World to Come: he that says the resurrection of the dead cannot be derived from the Torah; and he that says that the Torah is not from heaven; and a heretic" (Mishnah *Sanhedrin* 10). From this passage, we see that early rabbinic Judaism strongly embraced a belief in the afterlife. Yet the rabbis whose teachings are recorded in the Mishnah (known as *tannaim*, "teachers" or "repeaters") did not attempt to describe the "World to Come" in any great detail, as had the authors of the Pseudepigrapha, for example, in their depictions of heaven and hell. Instead, they maintained a consistent focus on the beliefs and behaviors that grant one a share in the World to Come or exclude one from it, as they sought to define normative Judaism in this period.

The Mishnah, an authoritative digest of oral laws codified about 200 C.E., contains the opinions of rabbis stretching across more than three centuries. Rabbi Judah ha-Nasi ("the Prince"), known simply as "Rabbi," is credited with arranging and redacting the various teachings. The text is divided into six orders, each dealing with a broad area of Jewish life. Interpreting and explaining the Hebrew Bible, this text presents the legal and theological system that came to be known as rabbinic Judaism. The Mishnah has remained the foundation stone of Jewish law up to the present. It therefore stands with the Hebrew Bible as one of two sacred texts upon which Judaism has been constructed.

In this chapter we will deal with resurrection and immortality as they appear in the Mishnah. We will also refer to other rabbinic texts of this period: the *Tosefta* ("additions") to the Mishnah, which are variant texts in the same format as the Mishnah that were not included in the codified edition, and the Midrash, writings generated from about 300 C.E. to the medieval period. *Midrashim* are rabbinic interpretations that fill in the gaps in biblical narrative, helping students of Bible understand references, laws, teachings, and events whose meanings are not apparent from reading biblical text alone.[1] Finally, we shall also refer to *Avot de-Rabbi Nathan,* a two-volume commentary written during the third century or later on Tractate *Avot* of the Mishnah.

That tractate, *Avot* (also known as *Pirke Avot,* "Sayings of the Fathers"),[2] is unique among the teachings of the Mishnah in that it contains no material that constitutes Jewish law, but rather moral and ethical teachings. In its very first paragraph, it affirms the divine origin and authority of the Written and Oral Law, tracing the "chain of tradition" that begins with Moses at Sinai and proceeds through the centuries to the rabbis of the Second Temple period, to Rabbi Yohanan ben Zakkai, and beyond. Thus it affirms the sacred nature of the Mishnah itself as Oral Law.

The Hebrew of the Mishnah is distinct from classical biblical Hebrew, employing a new, more flexible and technical Hebrew vocabulary. Among the new terms are two that are key to our study: *tehiyat ha-metim* ("resurrection of the dead")[3] and *olam ha-ba* ("the World to Come"), with "World to Come" the more prevalent expression.[4]

While the phrases *tehiyat ha-metim* and *olam ha-ba* firmly establish the early rabbis' belief in the resurrection of the dead and their expectation of the World to Come, the *tannaim* do not explore or analyze these concepts in as great detail as later rabbis in the Talmud. They do not venture to describe what the World to Come might look like or the possible mechanics of bodily resurrection. The rabbis of the Mishnah do believe, however, that all people will be judged and that there will be bodily resurrection, which is in some way connected with the World to

Come. This appears to be the ultimate reward of the individual Jew and also of the righteous gentile, according to some of the rabbis and later commentators. Even so, the rabbis of this period appear reluctant to describe what will happen in the World to Come or how the resurrection of the dead will take place.

One reason for this might be that the Mishnah is primarily a law code that leaves little room for speculation (although the Mishnah served more than that purpose for the rabbis, containing parables and aphorisms that illustrate and comment on human behavior as well). We cited in the previous chapter the passage from *Sanhedrin* in which the rabbis attempt to repress exploration of "external books" of the Apocrypha and the Pseudepigrapha. In the period after the destruction of the Temple by the Romans, it would have been a priority for the rabbis to preserve the authority of the canonized Bible. For that reason, they might have been reluctant to stray too far from its mainstream teachings. Since the hereafter is not a mainstream subject in the Hebrew Bible, these rabbis, too, might not have wished to overemphasize it. They regard it as important, but largely in terms of how belief in the hereafter influences day-to-day behavior.

HISTORICAL CONTEXT

In order to understand how and why ideas about the hereafter gained prominence in mainstream Jewish thought, we need to consider life during the Second Temple period, before the Mishnah was compiled. According to the historian Josephus, three sects that have an important bearing on our discussion are the Pharisees, the Sadducees, and the Essenes.[5] One theological concept that divided these sects was the nature of their belief in the hereafter, a difference in belief strong enough to direct the lives of each sect's followers in disparate directions. As we shall see, it is the teachings of the Pharisees that formed the foundation for most of later Jewish doctrine.

The Pharisees believed strongly in bodily resurrection and the immortality of the soul. Both doctrines grew naturally out of their belief that everything comes from God and that everything, including human destiny, is controlled by God's law. At the same time, another central element of Pharisaic teaching was the idea that human beings possess free will and are therefore capable of choosing whether to be righteous or wicked.[6] In other words, because God gave humans free will, they are accountable before God for their actions.

In *Antiquities of the Jews,* Josephus sums up the Pharisees' view of life after death:

> They also believe that souls have an immortal vigor in them and that under the earth there will be rewards or punishments according as they have lived virtuously or viciously in this life; and the latter are to be detained in an everlasting prison, but the former shall have the power to revive and live again. . . .[7]

This idea recalls the verse in Daniel (12:2) concerning resurrection, but here it has been expanded to mention the soul's "immortal vigor" and include an element of reward and punishment for the way people chose to live their lives. Physical resurrection is also apparently foreseen for the righteous. This promise of ultimate justice might help to explain the popularity of the Pharisees: the doctrine of an afterlife is a compelling answer to the problem of evil and would have been meaningful for Jews suffering under Roman domination.[8]

What distinguished the Pharisees from the other sects was their transmission not only of the written law, the Torah, but also the accompanying oral tradition and teachings. Josephus informs us that the Pharisees strove, in part through their skill in interpreting the law, to make Torah and tradition the supreme force in the life of the Jewish people. In this they were successful, achieving a high degree of popular support.[9]

The rabbis of the Mishnah do not explicitly identify themselves or their predecessors as Pharisees, but they embraced Pharisaic beliefs, such as the idea that behavior in this world affects the quality of one's existence in the afterlife. An opposing view on the life after death was held by the Sadducees, the priestly nobility. Josephus writes:

> The doctrine of the Sadducees is this: that souls die with
> the bodies; nor do they regard the observation of any
> thing besides what the [written] law enjoins them. ...
> This doctrine is received but by a few, yet by those still of
> the greatest dignity.[10]

Clearly, the Sadducees disagreed fundamentally with the Pharisees about the life hereafter, stating flatly that people's souls die with their bodies. While they also believed that humans had free will, they did not believe in reward or punishment for one's actions after death. In Josephus' opinion, the Saducean view led to a *laissez-faire* attitude about behavior.[11]

In this passage Josephus plainly states the Sadducees' rejection of the oral tradition in favor of what had been written (the written Torah).[12] He also shows the Sadducees' negative attitude toward the Pharisees, whom they regarded as upstarts and challengers to their inherited priestly status. The Sadducees were popular with some of the wealthy and politically powerful people in Jewish society,[13] but they did not obtain a "grassroots" following to rival that of the Pharisees.

The third sect, the Essenes, were an ascetic group that lived in the Judean desert. According to Josephus, the Essenes taught that the soul was immortal, being freed from the body at death and rising upwards to a heaven-like place:

> For their doctrine is this: That bodies are corruptible, and
> that the matter they are made of is not permanent; but
> that the souls are immortal, and continue for ever ... that
> when they are set free from the bonds of the flesh, they
> then, as released from a long bondage, rejoice and mount
> upward. Good souls have their habitations beyond the
> ocean, in a region that is neither oppressed with storms
> of rain or snow or with intense heat, but that this place
> is such as is refreshed by the gentle breathing of a west
> wind, blowing from the ocean; while they allot to bad
> souls a dark and tempestuous den, full of never-ceasing
> punishments.[14]

Although the Essenes believed in the immortality of the soul, and had highly developed ideas about where souls travel after death, they seemed to take no position on physical resurrection. Scholars are divided about what their actual belief was, as well as whether the Essenes were the sect or one of the sects that produced the Dead Sea Scrolls.[15]

Since the discovery of the Dead Sea Scrolls at Qumran in 1947, there have been numerous attempts to identify the sect that wrote them. Those scholars who ascribe the scrolls to Essene authorship make their case in part on the basis that they contain no references to physical resurrection. There are, however, isolated references to resurrection in the scrolls, which could suggest that the Essenes are not identical with the Dead Sea sect or that those parts of the literature were written by a different sect.

On the current evidence, at least two sets of Dead Sea Scroll fragments deal with the subject of resurrection. The first, called "The Messiah Apocalypse" or "The Messianic Apocalypse" is dated to 100 B.C.E. and provides insight into some of the early Jewish beliefs and traditions concerning the Messiah. In many other Dead Sea Scrolls we find mention of the Jewish hope for messianic redemption, usually coupled with the notion of redeemers who would restore Israel's past glory or usher in a utopian future. This passage from the Messiah Apocalypse is one of the few instances that speaks of God reviving the dead in the days of the Messiah:

> The heavens and the earth will listen to His messiah,
> And none therein will stray from the commandments of
>   the holy ones.
> Seekers of the Lord, strengthen yourselves in His service!
> All you hopeful in [your] heart, will you not find the
>   Lord in this?
> For the Lord will consider the pious and call the right-
>   eous by name.
> Over the poor His spirit will hover and will renew the
>   faithful with His power.
> And He will glorify the pious on the throne of the eternal
>   Kingdom.

> He who liberates the captives, restores sight to the blind,
>   straightens the bent . . . .
> And the Lord will accomplish glorious things . . . .
> For He will heal the wounded and revive the dead and
>   bring good news to the poor.
>
> (Dead Sea Scrolls, 4Q521, fragment 2)[16]

The second reference to resurrection is found in Pseudo-Ezekiel.[17] The writer of this scroll has modeled his work after the biblical book of Ezekiel and the text attaches itself to Ezekiel by quoting, rewriting, and enlarging on the biblical prophecies. In the scroll the narrator asks God how the righteous will be rewarded for their faith. The answer is a version of Ezekiel 37 in which the author gives an even more literal and explicit version of Ezekiel's vision of the dry bones as a prooftext for belief in the resurrection of the dead:[18]

> I have seen many from Israel who have loved Thy name and walked in the ways [of righteousness] . . . . How will their piety be rewarded? . . . [And He said,] "Son of man, prophesy concerning the bones, and say, 'Come together, a bone to its bone, and a bit [to its bit.]' " And so it came to pass. And He said a second time, "Prophesy, and let sinews come on them, and let skin spread over them above." And so it came to pass. And He said again, "Prophesy concerning the four winds of heaven, and let the winds of heaven blow [on them and they shall live]." And a great crowd of men revived and blessed the Lord of Hosts who made them live. And I said, "Lord, when will these things come to pass?" And the Lord said to me, ". . . a tree will bend and stand up . . . ."
>
> (Dead Sea Scrolls, 4Q385, fragment 2)[19]

In the passage above from the Messiah Apocalypse, the reference to God resurrecting the dead is clear: "He will heal the wounded and revive the dead . . . ." We also notice in the same passage that it is the pious that receive reward – a concept similar to that of the Pharisees' belief that those people who live virtuously will enjoy eternal life. Similarly, in the passage from Pseudo-Ezekiel, we see that it is the righteous whose bones will live again.

The question of whether these texts are of Essene authorship is outside the scope of this book, but the fact remains that a belief in resurrection is extant in some of the Dead Sea Scrolls. Resurrection, however, was an integral part of the Pharisaic viewpoint, which was adopted by the rabbis of the Mishnah and thereafter of the Talmud.[20]

WHAT DID THE RABBIS BELIEVE ABOUT THE WORLD TO COME?

Mishnah *Sanhedrin* 10, quoted at the beginning of this chapter, is the only passage in the Mishnah that mentions both the World to Come and resurrection. The dominant concept in this section however is the World to Come, as the passage first informs: "All Israel has a share in the World to Come." It then proceeds to declare that only those who hold the correct theological beliefs will attain a place there:

> All Israelites have a portion in the World to Come, for it is written: Thy people also shall be all righteous: they will inherit the land forever, the branch of my planting, the work of my hands, that I may be glorified. [Isaiah 60:21] But these people have no share in the World to Come: he that says the resurrection of the dead cannot be derived from the Torah; and he that says that the Torah is not from heaven; and a heretic.

In examining this passage, it is interesting to consider why the rabbis cited the prooftext from Isaiah. Most likely, the sages wanted to strengthen their reassurance to the people with the authority of Scripture that however dire their present circumstances were, they could always hope for improvement in a life beyond. It also might have been used to contest the allegation made by other sects, such as the early Christians, that the Jews would not be able to inherit eternal life. Here the rabbis present a text from within Jewish tradition, assuring its audience both of bodily resurrection and the World to Come.

A further question on this text might be: Why is the concept expressed as a "share" or a "portion" (*helek*) of the World to Come? Would it not be more reassuring to say that the whole of Israel is entitled to the whole of the World to Come? Perhaps the use of this term suggests that each person will receive what is due to him personally (like the midrash about the manna, which was considered to taste different to every individual).[21]

The rabbis set out numerous ways in which people can attain the World to Come – a desirable goal, because although we do not know where the World to Come is or what it contains, we know from the rabbis' teachings that it is a place we want to be. Perhaps we can also surmise, from the multiplicity of routes to it, that the features of the World to Come contain enough variety to bring eternal happiness to many different kinds of people.

After the Mishnah states who will attain the World to Come, it shifts to a discussion of who will be denied entry. If we look at the three categories of people who constitute exceptions, it is clear that, in contrast to the bulk of Jewish teachings which point to one's actions as the determinant of reward or punishment, *Sanhedrin* 10 contains several examples of *beliefs* that will disqualify people from admittance into the World to Come.

The Mishnah informs us that people can be excluded from the heritage owing to Israel (the World to Come) if they do not uphold the proper theological belief that resurrection is from the Torah and that the Torah is divine. In view of the differences among the sects discussed above, it becomes clear that this statement can be read as anti-Sadducee polemic, or at very least excluding those who read the law too narrowly to admit the possibility of resurrection. Finally, the heretic (*apikoros*) is excluded from the World to Come for his rejection of Jewish tradition.[22]

Few believing Jews would have disputed the divine nature of Torah. We may therefore surmise that by the time this passage was written, the requirement to believe in resurrection indicates that most Jews did, and those who did not were the minority. The rabbis appear to be acknowledging and supporting a widespread belief in resurrection.

It is clear from the text so far that resurrection and the World to Come are somehow related and that one cannot attain one's true inheritance – *olam ha-ba* – unless one also believes in resurrection.

Sanhedrin 10 continues:

> Rabbi Akiva says: Also he who reads heretical books: and he who whispers over a wound and says, "I will put none of the diseases on you which I have put on the Egyptians, for I am the Lord who heals you." Abba Saul says: Also he who pronounces the Divine Name as it is written.

Again, we see the rabbis stressing belief over action, indicating that heretics, believers in superstition, and blasphemers (like the one in the passage above who impersonates God) will also be denied a share in the World to Come. It is interesting to note that in this Mishnah the rabbis do not tie access to the World to Come to study, adherence to the commandments, or good deeds; neither do they promise entry to those who act well, or warn people who fail to study, follow the commandments, or carry out good works that they will be excluded.[23]

The chapter goes on to give multiple illustrations of specific people who will not attain the World to Come:

> Three kings and four commoners have no share in the World to Come. Three kings are Jeroboam and Ahab and Manasseh .... Four commoners are Balaam and Doeg and Ahitophel and Gehazi.

At this point, failure to earn a portion in the World to Come *is* based on bad behavior. Jeroboam, Ahab, and Manasseh, whose reigns are described in 1 and 2 Kings, were idolaters. Balaam was hired to curse the Israelites in the wilderness (Num. 22:1–24:25). Doeg assisted King Saul in exterminating supporters of David (1 Samuel 18–22). Ahitophel betrayed David in the war against his son Absalom (2 Samuel 15:12).

Finally, Gehazi, one of Elisha's students, ignored the prophet's order to not to take money for an act of healing (2 Kings 5).

The Mishnah then lists several groups of people mentioned in Torah who will not inherit the World to Come: the generation of the flood, the generation dispersed after building the Tower of Babel, the men of Sodom, the spies who brought a negative report to the Israelites in the wilderness, the entire generation of the wilderness, and the people of any town in the Promised Land who promote multiple gods. All these groups have in common a rebellious attitude against God.

We may wonder: why did the rabbis go into such detail about all these categories of sinners? The chapter begins by promising life hereafter to all Israel, but with the stipulation that its inhabitants adhere to a particular set of beliefs. However, as the sages enumerate all the people in the past history of the Jews who are disqualified from entry into the World to Come, their exclusion is based not only on their failure to believe properly but to behave properly, engaging in acts such as idolatry, betrayal, and inhospitality. As we can see, behavior as well as belief becomes an important criterion for entry into the World to Come.

WHAT DID THE RABBIS BELIEVE ABOUT RESURRECTION OF THE DEAD?

Along with the passing reference to resurrection in *Sanhedrin* 10:1, there are discussions of resurrection in these mishnaic tractates: Mishnah *Berakhot* 5:2, *Sotah* 9:15, and *Avot* 4:29.

Even the brief reference in *Berakhot* is significant because it states that resurrection of the dead should be mentioned in the second paragraph of the Amidah, a prayer central to Jewish worship.[24] Its inclusion in the Amidah (which was composed prior to the destruction of the Second Temple and reached its final arrangement at Yavneh) shows that a belief in resurrection was already established long before the Mishnah was compiled.

The *Sotah* reference to resurrection in Chapter 9 is attributed to Pinhas ben Yair, who taught during the second century and is described in rabbinic sources as a scholar of exemplary piety, perhaps even exaggerated piety. No legal rulings remain in his name, only edifying teachings. The passage in *Sotah* reads like a saint's progress to purity:

> R. Pinhas b. Yair says: Heedfulness leads to cleanliness, cleanliness leads to purity and purity leads to abstinence, and abstinence leads to holiness, and holiness leads to humility, and humility leads to shunning sin, and the shunning of sin leads to saintliness, and saintliness leads to [the gift of] the Holy Spirit, and the Holy Spirit leads to the resurrection of the dead, and the resurrection of the dead shall come through Elijah of blessed memory.
>
> (*Sotah* 9:15)

In this passage, Rabbi Pinhas clearly ties the achievement of resurrection to behavior that is not only in general accordance with God's commandments but is transcendently pure and saintly. In this case, devoted heedfulness of God's word leads to actions of increasing holiness that are powerful enough to bring about resurrection of the dead and the messianic age.

The final reference in the Mishnah to resurrection is in *Pirke Avot*, the "Sayings of the Fathers." Although *Pirke Avot* contains many references to the World to Come, this passage is the only specific reference to resurrection in the entire tractate of *Avot*:

> He [R. Elazar ha-Kappar] used to say: Those who are born [are fated] to die, and those who die [are fated] to be brought to life, and [the resurrected] are destined to be judged, that man may know and make known and understand that He is God, He is the Fashioner, He is the Creator, He is the One Who understands, He is the Judge, He is the Witness, He is the One Who brings suit, He is the one who in the future will judge, Blessed be He, before whom there is no wrongdoing or forgetfulness, nor favoritism, nor bribe-taking. Know that everything

is according to its reckoning, and do not let your [own] inclination cause you to believe that Sheol is a refuge for you. For against your will you are formed, against your will you are born, and against your will you live, and against your will you die, and against your will you will have to give an account before God, the King of Kings, blessed be He.[25]

This passage is important because it is very specific about the judgment that will take place before one enters the World to Come. One idea leads to another: Because God's judgment is inescapable, it is not possible to pretend that Sheol is a refuge (or that everything will vanish into forgetfulness after one's death). One's life leads inexorably not only to death, but also to an accounting before God after one's death. Therefore, it is important to behave properly in this world so as to be able to render a proper account of one's behavior before God in the World to Come.

When we read all four references to resurrection in the Mishnah together, we can see that although individual references to bodily resurrection are few, the ideas have impact great enough to influence religious belief and practice to this day.

WHO WILL HAVE A SHARE IN THE WORLD TO COME?

Olam ha-ba, "the World to Come," was a favorite expression of the rabbis, but it is unclear where the term comes from. Although there is a similar expression in 1 Enoch 71:15 ("He will proclaim peace to you in the name of the world that is to become"), the rabbis, as we noted in the previous chapter, apparently did not approve of the Apocrypha and the Pseudepigrapha, so they may not have found the term in Enoch. It may never be known for certain whether the term was borrowed and, if so, by whom.

Along with the seventeen mentions of *olam ha-ba* in Tractate *Sanhedrin,* the phrase appears ten times in *Pirke Avot* with single references in *Peah, Kiddushin,* and *Bava Metzia.* In looking at all the references to *olam ha-ba* in the Mishnah, we can establish the importance of a concept of life after death in the minds of the *tannaim,* an importance that later rabbis will amplify and intensify in the Talmud. Although the discussion of *olam ha-ba* in *Sanhedrin* centers on who will be denied a place there rather than who will be admitted, in other passages of the Mishnah the rabbis set out positive pathways to the World to Come based on lifestyle and good works.

Torah Study

The great sage Hillel, who lived during the first century B.C.E., was the first to say that by studying Torah, a person acquired life in the World to Come.[26] He was followed by a galaxy of scholars stressing the importance of Torah study as a way of achieving the World to Come, a concept that is a cornerstone of rabbinic Judaism to this day. At the same time, Hillel warned that Torah study was not to be used for self-aggrandizement: "One who makes worldly use of the crown [of Torah] shall pass away."[27]

Rabbi Tarfon, who taught during the first part of the second century C.E., adopted Hillel's teaching, stressing that those who study a great deal of Torah receive their reward in the "time to come" (*atid la-vo*).[28] Rabbi Zadok, a contemporary of Rabbi Tarfon, repeated Hillel's admonition against making worldly use of Torah, warning not only to avoid making Torah a crown for oneself, a way to inflate one's self-importance, but also admonishing the student not to make it "a spade wherewith to dig,"[29] meaning that one must make the study of Torah an end in itself, not the means to one's livelihood. In other words, one must study for the love of Torah itself. Many of the sages worked jobs in the secular world as artisans and even laborers so that their study time would represent *Torah lishma,* "Torah for its own sake."

By making these assertions, the rabbis are reformulating the ideal of Torah study. As some scholars have suggested, Torah study would logically seem to be confined to a human lifespan; once people are dead, they have discharged their human function and cannot learn Torah any more. Here, though, the rabbis are extending the concept of Torah so that it becomes a bridge into the World to Come. Rabbi Yose ben Kisma, another contemporary of Rabbi Tarfon, uses Proverbs to support his refusal to leave his "great city of sages and scribes" (that is, of dedicated Torah study), even for an exorbitant offer of wealth, because his learning is the only thing that will accompany him in the hereafter:

> But in the hour of man's departure neither silver nor gold nor jewels nor pearls accompany him but only Torah and good deeds, as it is said: "When you walk it will lead you, when you lie down it will watch over you and when you awake it will talk to you" [Proverbs 6:22]. When you walk it will lead you: in this world; when you lie down it will watch over you: in the grave; and when you awake it will talk with you: in the World to Come.[30]   (*Avot* 6:9)

"The Labor of Your Hands"

For other sages, the study of Torah is not the only endeavor that enables admittance to the hereafter. Ben Zoma, a disciple of rabbis during the second century C.E., is best known as one of the four sages in the Talmud (Ben Azzai, Ben Zoma, Aher, and Rabbi Akiva) who entered the mystical orchard (*pardes*) to solve the mysteries of the world; only Akiva, according to legend, emerged unscathed.[31]

Here Ben Zoma adds a new dimension to the conversation of the hereafter by claiming that the honest labor of a person's hands will give entrance to the World to Come. Although he implies that study is essential for the attainment of wisdom ("Who is wise? He who learns from all men"), Ben Zoma mentions the World to Come only when he answers the question "Who is rich?"

> He who rejoices in his portion, as it is said, "When you eat the labor of your hands, you will be happy and good [will come] to you." [Psalms 128:2] "You will be happy" – in this world; "and good will come to you" – in the World to Come.   (*Avot* 4:1)

Clearly, Ben Zoma views work, and not just Torah study, as a way to gain entry to life hereafter. If we add Ben Zoma's egalitarian perspective to Hillel's teaching, there is a place in the World to Come not only for the Torah scholar but for the honest laborer as well.

Good Deeds

Rabbi Yose ben Kisma taught that not only Torah but also good deeds survive past death and into the World to Come: "At the time a person dies neither silver nor gold nor jewels nor pearls accompany him but only Torah and good deeds. . . ." (*Avot* 6:9).[32] Those good deeds are summarized in Mishnah *Peah,* which is quoted in the traditional morning service:

> These are the things where no measure is prescribed . . . deeds of lovingkindness and the study of the law. These are things whose fruits a man enjoys in this world while the capital is laid up for him in the World to Come: honoring father and mother, deeds of loving kindness, making peace between a man and his fellow, and the study of the Torah is equal to them all.   (Mishnah *Peah* 1:1)

Self-Denial

Although Judaism does not have a strong tradition of asceticism or self-denial, one teaching found in *Avot* promotes privation as an appropriate lifestyle for Torah study:

> This is the way that is becoming to the study of Torah: eat bread with salt, and drink water by measure, sleep on the ground, and live a life of deprivation while you toil in the Torah. If you do this, "you will be happy, and good [will come] to you" in the World to Come.   (*Avot* 6:4)

The anonymous sage who contributed this idea quotes the same verse from Psalms 128:2 that Ben Zoma uses to support his argument that physical labor brings a reward in the hereafter. In this passage, however, the quotation from Psalms is used to promise a place in the World to Come based on self-restraint and ascetic behavior.

This notion (along with Rabbi Pinhas ben Yair's connection of abstinence and holiness in Tractate *Sotah,* cited above) diverges from mainstream Judaism which, generally speaking, does not see the study of Torah and the enjoyment of creature comforts as mutually exclusive. In fact, in the Jerusalem Talmud, the rabbis state that when brought to judgment, human beings will have to account before God for every legitimate pleasure they denied themselves (*Kiddushin* 4:12). Tractate *Avot* of the Mishnah itself advocates a middle ground between the two positions when it declares *Im ein kemah ein Torah* – "Without meal [that is, worldly sustenance], there is no Torah" (*Avot* 3:21).[33]

Indeed, according to multiple commentators, the lesson in *Avot* 6:4 is not that self-denial is the *only* way in which Torah should be acquired, but that it is possible to study Torah under harsh conditions and that such study will be rewarded greatly. The great medieval scholar, Rashi (1140–1205), understood the passage to mean that poverty is not an excuse for failing to study Torah, saying, "It does not mean that a rich man should live under these privations to study the Torah. It means that even if a man has no more than a slice of bread with salt . . . even he must not abstain from studying, because in the end he will study when being wealthy."[34]

Keeping the Commandments

From the Midrash comes another path to the hereafter:

> "You shall keep my laws and my rules, by the pursuit of which man shall live" (Lev. 18:5) – in the World to Come. And should you wish to claim that the reference is to this world, is it not the fact that in the end one dies? Lo, how am I to explain, "shall live"? It is with reference to the World to Come . . . .[35]

Here, the sages promise that observance of God's commandments will guarantee entry to the World to Come. While other texts specifically cite Torah study or good works as paths to the hereafter, this midrash presents a mandate that encompasses both study and acts of kindness and much more besides: to be observant of all God's *mitzvot,* a rather high hurdle to jump. Once again, the categories for entry to the World to Come are being extended with the purpose of promoting correct behavior and ensuring that as many Jews as possible attain the hereafter.

WHO WILL BE EXCLUDED FROM THE WORLD TO COME?

An explanation of how *not* to enter the World to Come is expressed by Rabbi Elazar of Modi'in, who taught in the early second century C.E. and was murdered during the Bar Kokhba revolt (132–135 C.E.).[36]

> He who defiles sacred things, scorns the festivals, publicly shames his neighbor, nullifies the covenant of our father Abraham, and interprets the Torah not according to *halakhah* [Jewish law] – even if he has learning and good deeds to his credit – has no portion in the future world. (*Avot* 3:15)

This passage can refer to several different types of people who were estranging themselves from rabbinic Judaism in the period following the destruction of the Second Temple:

- Assimilationist Jews who had adopted the mores of the dominant Greco-Roman culture.
- Sectarian Jews who rejected the authority of the rabbis.
- Judeo-Christians, who were no longer observing Jewish rituals and festivals.

Rabbi Elazar implies that exclusion from the World to Come can be based either on lapses of belief or behavior. The person who interprets

Torah out of accordance with *halakhah* does not believe in the divine origin of the law. As a heretic, he cannot attain the World to Come even if he studies and performs acts of kindness. On the other hand, the public shaming or humiliation of one's fellow man, a profoundly unethical act, also removes the perpetrator from the ranks of those worthy of attaining the World to Come, belief in Torah notwithstanding.[37] Clearly, the rabbis required both belief in God's word and righteous behavior for attainment of the World to Come.

Avot de-Rabbi Nathan, as we mentioned earlier, is a commentary on Mishnah *Avot.* Scholars are in dispute about its exact dating; it has been preserved in two versions, and while its earliest passages may date from the late tannaitic period, various commentators place its compilation at anywhere from fifty to five hundred years after the Mishnah was codified. While the ideas about the afterlife expounded in *Avot de-Rabbi Nathan* are substantially the same as in the Mishnah, there is one additional idea found only in the B or second version. Rabbi Yose, the student of Rabbi Akiva, attempts to address the age-old issue of theodicy – the question of why there is so much suffering in the world in the presence of a just God:

> A righteous man for whom life goes well: [this is] a righteous man who is the son of a righteous man. His deeds are good and his ancestors' deeds were good. His ancestors' deeds entitle him to success in this world: and by his own deeds he will secure for himself the right to eat in the World to Come.
>
> A righteous man for whom life goes badly: this is a righteous man who is the son of an evil man. His own deeds are good, but those of his ancestors were not. His ancestors have not entitled him to eat in this world, but he will entitle himself to eat in the World to Come.
>
> An evil man for whom life goes well: this is an evil man who is the son of a righteous man. His own deeds are not good, but those of his ancestors were. His ancestors entitled him to eat in this world, but he will not entitle himself to eat in the World to Come.

> An evil man for whom life goes badly: this is an evil man who is the son of an evil man. His ancestors did not entitle him to eat in this world and he will not entitle himself to eat in the World to Come.[38]

Here we see the struggle of the rabbis to explain why good people suffer, using ancestors' bad behavior as a way of explaining one's troubles in this world while making clear that it is one's own actions that will grant or deny entry to the World to Come. The role of the individual's behavior in securing his own destiny is critical. The merit of one's ancestors has influence only in this world; it counts for nothing in the World to Come, which can be secured only by one's own efforts.

The Mishnah never tells us exactly what the World to Come looks like or how people will live there. Yet it stresses that this life (*olam ha-zeh*) is only a preliminary to another, higher life. Though the rabbis do not use extensive imagery in portraying what happens inside the heavens, as the apocalyptic literature does, they do express a belief that the World to Come will be a perfect world, without suffering or injustice. Rabbi Jacob ben Korshai, who belonged to the fourth generation of sages, described the difference between this world and the World to Come somewhat paradoxically:

> Better one hour of repentance and good deeds in this world than all the World to Come; better one hour of calmness of spirit in the World to Come than all the life of this world. (*Avot* 4:22)

As blissful as the World to Come may be, Rabbi Jacob reminds us, one must not denigrate this world because only in this world can one do the meritorious deeds that will allow one to attain the World to Come. "This world is like a vestibule before the World to Come," he taught. "Prepare yourself in the vestibule so that you may enter the banquet hall."[39]

The Talmud: What Happens in the Next World?

THE RABBIS OF the Mishnah were eager to add a practical, behavioral element to their treatment of the World to Come, thus ensuring that Jews of the time would have an incentive to behave correctly and follow God's commandments. While they sought to maintain Jewish law in this world with the promise of reward in the next, they generally refrained from puzzling out the details of what the World to Come would be like. This changes in the later part of the rabbinic era as the sages of the Talmud fleshed out their notions of the hereafter and expanded upon these important theological ideas. Jumping in where the Mishnah leaves off, they developed specific concepts about what happens in the hereafter: places of reward (*Gan Eden*) and punishment (*Gehinnom*), resurrection, and the World to Come. They also explored the relationship of the soul to the body, an idea that the earlier rabbis did not address. Taken in sum, the rabbis of the Talmud established the landscape in which all further discussions about the life hereafter in Jewish tradition would take place.

The Talmud is a commentary on the Mishnah that records the discussions of generations of sages over a period of roughly three hundred years after the Mishnah was codified. These discussions deal with social and religious conduct, Torah study, and how Jews should relate to the outside world – especially now that a sizable number of Jews were living outside of the Land of Israel. More than two thousand talmudic commentators called *amoraim* ("those who interpret") are quoted by name in the Talmud.

The text of the Talmud includes both the Mishnah and the commentary of the *amoraim* upon it. This commentary, known as the Gemara ("completion"), explores the text of the Mishnah in great detail. The rabbis use biblical citations, alternative teachings, and contemporary references to explicate the mishnaic texts as they wrestle with what they mean and how they affect Jewish life. Contradictory ideas and disparate interpretations are treated with respect; a page of Gemara might record vastly differing views about an issue, yet none is omitted. The Talmud is a wide-ranging compendium of ideas with no systematic format because links are made associatively. This makes the Talmud a particularly challenging work to navigate. Indeed, it is often called the "Sea of Talmud."

There are in fact two Talmuds. The earlier, known as the Jerusalem Talmud, records the discussions conducted in the academies of the Land of Israel under Roman rule. Other scholars fled to Babylonia after the destruction of the Second Temple and established academies there. From those academies came the Babylonian Talmud, which is much longer than the Jerusalem Talmud, reaching its final form in approximately 500 C.E., although rabbis called the *saboraim*, "expositors," contributed some explanatory notes and did the final editing over the next two hundred years. Of the two, the Babylonian Talmud, known also as the Bavli, is better known and cited more often.[1]

The rabbinical sages of the Talmud discuss the hereafter frequently, although, true to the talmudic method, they are not systematic in the way they present the material. Nevertheless, the work of the rabbis of this period substantially develops the doctrines relating to resurrection and the World to Come and delineates the relationship between the body and the immortal soul. Many of their ideas contradict each other. In fact, any attempt to systematize their notions of the afterlife imposes upon them an order and a consistency they do not have. Their religious significance lies in the definitive establishment of a belief in the afterlife, as witnessed by the variety of ways in which the sages imagined it.

Despite the many views recorded, certain general features stand out:

that there is judgment after death; that righteous souls are rewarded in *Gan Eden* and wicked ones punished in *Gehinnom*; that the dead will be resurrected in the days of the Messiah; and that the righteous will live on in *olam ha-ba*, "the World to Come." The sequence of these events, however, is acknowledged to be a mystery filled with unanswerable questions and openings for speculation.

𝕬   HOW IS RESURRECTION POSSIBLE?

One obvious question that the Mishnah did not address is: How can a reasonable person believe in resurrection? Dead people are dead; how can they be brought back to life? The *amoraim* of the Talmud propose a number of solutions to show that resurrection is not only possible but will be a miraculous process similar to the mystery of birth.

Resurrection was important to the rabbis because, like creation, it exemplifies God's power; it is one of the reasons believing Jews say *ha-kol yachol* – God can do everything. To deny God's ability to resurrect the dead was to deny God's omnipotence, so belief in resurrection became an article of faith, the denial of which was not only condemned as sinful but would bar the denier from entering the World to Come.[2] As we shall see, the rabbis of the Talmud endeavored to show that resurrection is no more miraculous than birth or the annual revival of plant life after winter. In the same way as life is generated by God, it can be regenerated by God.

Among the stories in the Talmud (*aggadot,* or rabbinic tales) we find an anonymous emperor allegedly saying to Rabban Gamaliel II (a sage of the princely house during the mishnaic period, 90–115 C.E.): "The dead are like dust. How can they be resurrected?" It is the emperor's daughter who answers by comparing two artisans, one who creates from water and one from clay. "Who is more praiseworthy?" she asks, setting the stage for the rabbi's reply. Rabban Gamaliel responds: "The one who creates from water is more praiseworthy, as it is more difficult to shape items out of water." "Exactly," the emperor's daughter concurs, and substituting another liquid medium, semen, for water, she says: "If [God] can make man from water [sperm], surely He can do so from clay!" (*Sanhedrin* 90b–91a).[3]

The point of the parable, of course, is that God can do anything, but it also goes on to suggest that resurrection will not involve creating new people from dust. That was the pattern for the original creation of man: "The Lord God formed man from the dust of the earth. He blew into his nostrils the breath of life, and man became a living being" (Genesis 2:7). Other passages in the Talmud also suggest that this process will not be repeated for the resurrection. Instead, there will be some other undefined, natural phenomenon that is similar to actual birth.

The argument of the emperor's daughter is reinforced with a number of similar arguments about resurrection, none of which suggests any process that resembles the original creation. Rabbi Ammi, for example, is alleged to have shown, by referring to the way that snails proliferate after rain, that God is capable of creating large amounts of life very rapidly. This section of the discussion concludes with a *min* ("sectarian")[4] asking Gebiha ben Pesisa:[5] "Living people die, so how can the dead live?" Gebiha answers: "If something that was not alive [i.e., a fetus] can become alive, surely the dead can live again" (*Sanhedrin* 91a). Once again, the analogy is with birth, not with creation.

The process of resurrection is compared to the restorative qualities of rain in another reference involving water. Along with the instruction to praise God for "giving life to the dead" in the second paragraph of the Amidah, the rabbis of the Mishnah (*Berakhot* 5:2) prescribed that worshipers invoke God's power to make rain fall during the winter months. In *Berakhot* 33a, Rabbi Joseph is recorded as stating that the reason for this is that rain is deemed to be equivalent to resurrection. Just as God is capable of reviving the dead, God is capable of reviving the thirsty ground with rain.[6]

An elegantly constructed argument for resurrection from Tractate *Sanhedrin* cites a list from Proverbs of things that will never be satisfied – the grave, the barren womb, the parched earth, and fire – and compares them:

> Rabbi Tabi said in Rabbi Yosia's name: What is meant by "Sheol [the grave], and the barren womb, and the earth that is not sated with water, and fire never say 'Enough!'"

(Proverbs 30:16) – now, what connection does the grave have with the womb? But it is to teach you: just as the womb receives and brings forth, so does the grave too receive and bring forth .... [H]ere is a refutation for those who deny that resurrection is taught in the Torah.

(*Sanhedrin* 92a)[7]

It appears from these texts that, despite the objections of various non-believers, resurrection will be natural, straightforward and spontaneous, an image borne out several times by the rabbis. It is noteworthy that one of the arguments for resurrection is attributed to a woman (the emperor's daughter) and another to a layperson who is also disabled (Gebiha ben Pesisa was a hunchback), as if to underscore the idea that not only rabbis and scholars, but also ordinary people, believed in the revival of the dead. The presence of a woman in these texts also subtly serves to reinforce the analogy the rabbis are attempting to draw between resurrection and birth.

Resurrection was a central doctrine in the Mishnah, which declared that any person who denied that resurrection was derived from Torah (in this context, the five books of Moses) would lose his place in the World to Come. But the Mishnah, where in so many places sages quote the *Tanakh* (the Hebrew Bible) to support their assertions, provides no prooftexts in regard to resurrection other than Isaiah 26:19 and Daniel 12:2, where resurrection is mentioned explicitly. On the other hand, the rabbis of the Talmud, charged with explicating statements in the Mishnah, come up with numerous biblical citations regarding resurrection that are less direct but nonetheless ingenious and persuasive. Again, a number of these answers are framed as responses by the rabbis to *minim* ("sectarians") and other challengers to rabbinic authority.

One example is Rabban Gamaliel's extended conversation with some persistent non-believers in afterlife and resurrection (*Sanhedrin* 90b). According to the passage, they ask Rabban Gamaliel, "Whence do we know that the Holy One, Blessed be He, will resurrect the dead?" The rabbi attempts to bring answers from all three sections of *Tanakh* – Torah, Prophets, and Writings.

Gamaliel's opening tactic is to try to prove resurrection is from the

Torah itself. He reportedly cites Deuteronomy 31:16 as reading: "You will lie down with your fathers and rise." The *minim* do not accept this, noting that in the verse, Moses, near death, is about to lie down with his fathers, but it is the people Israel who will rise and, as God predicts, follow alien gods in their new land.

Undeterred, Gamaliel continues, quoting Isaiah 26:19: "Let your dead live! Corpses shall arise; awake and sing, you who live in the dust." This is a much more convincing text for resurrection, but the *minim* refuse to accept it, arguing that the Isaiah reference is to the revival of the "dry bones" in Ezekiel 37. The *minim* argue that God may have conjured a field full of skeletons back to life in this instance, but it was a one-time event, a sort of magic trick that does not predict any future resurrection. In other words, they lack faith in an all-powerful God that can resurrect the dead again and again.

The biblical prophet Ezekiel preached during the exile of the Hebrews in Babylonia during the sixth century B.C.E., and the vision of the dry bones takes place in the context of his hope that his people would eventually reclaim their land (a prophecy that in fact came true when Jews were allowed to return from Babylonia). The rabbis in *Sanhedrin* 92b however take the image of the revived dead of Ezekiel 37 literally and argue that even if it were a one-time event, it proves that resurrection is possible. Some of the rabbis speculate that the revival that took place was brief, with Rabbi Eliezer allegedly asserting, "[They] stood up on their feet, uttered a song and died." But an argument attributed to another Eliezer, Rabbi Eliezer ben (son of) Rabbi Yose the Galilean, states that Ezekiel's dead married and had descendants after entering the land of Israel. Rabbi Yehuda ben Bathyra then announces that he is one of those descendants, displaying his grandfather's *tefillin* (phylacteries) as proof. The rabbis go on to debate exactly who were the people resurrected from the dry bones, never resolving the question of whether the revival was fleeting or permanent. Nevertheless, it is clear that they see the resurrection of these dead as a miracle that establishes the paradigm for resurrection.

Gamaliel finally convinces the *minim* by citing Deuteronomy 11:21: "In the land [God] swore to your fathers to give them." Because the text says, "give *them*" and not "give *you*," this implies they will be resurrected in order to enjoy the Promised Land. As further proof, Gamaliel quotes Deuteronomy 4:4: "You who held fast to [God] are all alive today"; that is, just as you are alive today, you will live in the World to Come.

Other rabbis bring similar arguments in this part of Tractate *Sanhedrin*: for example, that in order for Aaron to receive his prescribed tithe, he must be resurrected (90b), or that the patriarchs need to be resurrected in order to be given the land personally as promised.

Another line of argument to which a number of rabbis subscribe states that when a text contains a verb in the imperfect tense, although it refers to an action that has already occurred, it should be understood as a reference to future resurrection. Rabbi Meir is recorded as citing the Song at the Sea (Exodus 15:1): "Then Moses sang [*yashir*] to God." He understands the imperfect tense – used here even though the sentence is always translated in the past tense – to refer to something that will happen in the future and therefore to resurrection (Tractate *Sanhedrin* 91b). He and other rabbis go on to read other texts containing imperfect verbs, often referring to praise or song, in a similar way.

A further category of argument is to read repetitions or duplications of verbs, employed often in the Bible for emphasis, as referring to the action occurring twice, once in this world and once in the next. For example, when the Bible says in Numbers 15:31 that someone who rejects God's word and violates God's commandments "shall be cut off, cut off," the rabbis read that as "cut off in this world and cut off in the next" (*Sanhedrin* 90b). Similarly, in *Sanhedrin* 92a, Rava teaches that the phrase "Let Reuben live and not die" (Deut. 33:6) should be interpreted with "live" referring to this world and "not die" referring to the next. Thus the verse not only expresses a wish for the here and now, but also a desire that Reuben (both the individual and the Israelite tribe that carries his name) enjoy the life hereafter.

It is possible that the rabbis focus on this statement in particular because it is part of Moses' deathbed address to the congregation of Israel. Perhaps they thought it was a final reminder by Moses to the people that his leadership would continue in the World to Come. This argument is supported by the next teaching in the Talmud, attributed to Rabbi Eleazar, who states: "Every leader who leads the community with mildness will be privileged to lead them in the next world [too]" (*San-hedrin* 92b).

Rava, a Babylonian sage, explicitly links resurrection to God's powers as described in the Torah:

> Our Rabbis taught: "I kill and I make alive" [Deut. 32:39].
> I might interpret: I kill one person and give life to another,
> as is the way of the world, so the [biblical] text states:
> "I wound and I heal." Just as the wounding and healing
> obviously refer to the same person, so putting to death
> and bringing to life refer to the same person. This refutes
> those who maintain that resurrection is not intimated in
> the Torah. (*Sanhedrin* 91b)

Finally, the rabbis turn to the recognizably eschatological texts from Daniel that refer explicitly to resurrection:

> Rabina said: [Resurrection] is derived from this verse:
> And many of them that sleep in the dust of the earth shall
> awake, some to everlasting life, and some to shame and
> everlasting contempt [Daniel 12:2]. R. Ashi said: From
> this verse: But you will go until the end; then you will
> rest, and then you will rise for your destiny at the end of
> days [Daniel 12:13]. (*Sanhedrin* 92a)

As we have seen, the *amoraim* were intent upon showing that resurrection and the afterlife were very much present, if not immediately apparent, topics in the Bible. Indeed, in an early midrash, Rabbi Simai is recorded as stating: "There is no *parshah* [weekly portion] in the Torah that does not deal with the resurrection of the dead, but we do not have the strength [or ability] to explain it" (*Sifre* Deut. 306).

The significance of this effort to implant a belief in the hereafter, and particularly in resurrection, was to convince people of the reality of reward and retribution after death: Even if one did not attain one's reward here on earth, one would undoubtedly receive it beyond this life.

✿   JUDGMENT, REWARD, AND PUNISHMENT

The rabbis clearly conceived that there would be some process by which individuals were required to account after death for their behavior on earth.[8] The underlying idea was that since God is just, God will requite people fairly for their behavior. Hence, the righteous are rewarded for their faith and the wicked punished for their rebellion and disbelief. Then, as now, it was often the case that reward or punishment did not transpire in a person's lifetime. The idea of retribution after death neatly solves this dilemma.[9]

The process begins with the individual being called to account:

> [The Rabbis] said: When a man departs to his eternal home, all his deeds are enumerated before him and he is told, such and such a thing have you done, in such and such a place on that particular day. And he replies, Yes. Then they say to him, Sign. And he signs . . . . And what is more, he acknowledges the justice of the verdict, and he says, "You have judged me well."   (*Ta'anit* 11a)

In some places, the Talmud specifies additional questions to be asked of those waiting for judgment. For example, in *Shabbat* 31a, the rabbis envision the following examination: "Did you deal with integrity? Did you fix times for learning? Did you generate a family? Did you wait for redemption? Did you engage in wise debate? Did you infer one thing from another?" Some of these questions are easier to understand than others. For example, we can see that the rabbis of this period wanted to require people to be honest, studious, and productive, suggesting that they will be questioned about their integrity, study, and procreativity when they come to judgment. The other three questions deal with the more nebulous categories of faith, interpersonal relations, and intelligence, but they make clear that the rabbis also prized qualities such as the patience to wait for the Messiah to come, as well as common sense and the ability to get along with others.

After the judgment, dead persons are sent to the destinations deemed appropriate by their deeds in life. Rabbi Yohanan ben Zakkai's death scene in *Berakhot* 28b describes the alternatives: *Gehinnom* (roughly equivalent to hell) and *Gan Eden* (paradise).

Rabbi Yohanan's disciples come to visit when he is ill and ask why he is weeping. He replies that it would be appropriate to weep if he were being led before a human king who might punish him, but whom perhaps he could bribe and appease: how much more so, he asks, when he is being led into the presence of the Holy One, who lives and endures for all eternity, who could punish him forever, and who cannot be bribed? He says: "When before me lie two ways, one of *Gan Eden* and one of *Gehinnom*, and I know not to which I am to be led, shall I not weep?" *Gan Eden* and *Gehinnom*, then, come to symbolize reward and punishment in the afterlife.[10]

Gan Eden

Although the rabbis call the destination of the righteous "the Garden of Eden," it is clear that they do not mean the same location as the earthly garden in which Adam, the first human, was placed.[11] Instead they envisage an environment in which the righteous will enjoy the rich benefits that they earned but may have been denied on earth. They will feast on the flesh of the Leviathan, the sea monster mentioned in Isaiah, Psalms, and Job and will experience the joy of being in the divine presence of God:

> In the days to come the Holy Blessed One will arrange a dance for the righteous in the Garden of Eden, with Him sitting among them, and each will point to Him with his finger, saying, "This is our God, we have waited for Him and He will save us . . . ." (*Ta'anit* 31a)

When not celebrating, the righteous will dwell according to their rank, which is determined by their piety:

> Every righteous person is given a habitation as befits his honor. This might be compared to a king who enters a

town with his servants. They all go in through the same
gate, but when they spend the night there, each is given a
lodging befitting his rank. (*Shabbat* 152a)

In addition, *Gan Eden* is seen as being particularly hospitable to
scholars. Those who were intellectually troubled on earth will be given
the answers to the problems they could not solve there:

The words *asher kummetu* [lit., "those who press forward"] indicate blessing: these are the scholars who
wrinkle [their brows] over the words of the Torah in this
world, which is why the Holy Blessed One will reveal a
secret to them in the World to Come. (*Hagigah* 14a)

In sum, *Gan Eden* is regarded by the rabbis of the Talmud as being
a place of eternal happiness and pleasure, a destination those who were
righteous in life can look forward to after death.

Gehinnom

According to the rabbis, God designed *Gehinnom* even before He formed
the world (*Pesahim* 54a). Scanning the biblical text for references to
the underworld, the sages extract seven names for it: Sheol, Perdition,
Destruction, Roaring Pit, Slimy Clay, Shadow of Death and Nether-world
(*Eruvin* 19a). They also discuss where the physical entrance to the underworld is located, some rabbis holding that it has three entrances (one in
the wilderness, one in the sea, and one in Jerusalem), and others locating
a single entrance from which smoke ascends between two date palms in
the valley of Beth Hinnom. The name *Gehinnom* derives from *gei ben hinnom*, a valley outside the Western Wall of Jerusalem in which refuse was
dumped and corpses had been burned in pagan sacrifices.

Gehinnom is envisioned as having seven levels.[12] It is a realm of fire,
brimstone, smoke, and darkness, where a stream of fire issues from
beneath God's throne and breaks upon the heads of the wicked.[13] The
fire is of abnormal intensity, with the rabbis saying in *Berakhot* 57b that
"[ordinary] fire is a sixtieth of the fire of *Gehinnom*."

Here and there the rabbis state that this or that type of person "will inherit *Gehinnom*" as an expression of extreme disapproval. They do not appear to envisage, though, that people will have to stay there permanently. A long passage beginning in *Rosh ha-Shanah* 16b describes how the thoroughly righteous will be sent to *Gan Eden* and the thoroughly wicked to *Gehinnom* (citing the now-familiar passage from Daniel 12:2). Those called *benonim* ("in-betweeners") who are neither completely righteous nor bad, however, will go down to *Gehinnom* and then rise again.[14] In *Eruvin* 19a, the sages describe a scenario in which wicked persons are sentenced temporarily to *Gehinnom* but, except for the worst offenders, they are brought up from there by the patriarch Abraham who receives them in *Gan Eden*.

The rabbis also consider the question of how long the wicked will remain in *Gehinnom*. The majority, they say in *Rosh ha-Shanah* 17a, will spend a year in Sheol and then their bodies will be destroyed, their souls burned and their ashes scattered under the feet of the righteous. In other words, their torment will end. Conversely, a number of categories of people will be punished in *Gehinnom* "for all generations." These include sectarians (those who rejected the Torah and denied the resurrection of the dead), those who led others to sin, and other unredeemable wrong-doers. These categories are very similar to those we considered in our study of Mishnah *Sanhedrin* earlier, but their punishment has become much more explicit. Not only will these people not inherit a share in the World to Come, but they will suffer torment throughout eternity.

The sages do identify several ways during life to avoid *Gehinnom*. One is the recitation of certain prayers, including the *Sh'ma,* the statement of God's sovereignty and oneness (*Berakhot* 15b); another is repentance of one's sins. The most effective safeguard against the fire of *Gehinnom*, however, is Torah study; in *Hagigah* 27a, we are told that Israelites who are filled with Torah "as a pomegranate is filled with seeds" will be able to resist the fire. In the Midrash (Genesis Rabbah 11:5), we learn that those sentenced to *Gehinnom* are relieved of their suffering every Sabbath.[15]

We should note how much more developed the concept of the underworld as a place of pain and punishment becomes in the talmudic period. The torments forced on people in *Gehinnom* reflected the cruel punishments practiced by the Roman government. The descriptions of fiery torment and bodily mutilation in turn influenced early Christian views of punishment in the netherworld and, indeed, read more like the modern idea of Hell than what we saw in the shadowy half-life of the biblical Sheol.

Olam ha-ba, the World to Come

The reward for living a righteous life is a share in *olam ha-ba,* "the World to Come," an expression the rabbis use to describe both the afterlife (sometimes used interchangeably with *Gan Eden*) and the world that will follow the days of the Messiah. Though vague about its precise meaning, the sages of the Talmud speculate about what the World to Come will be like. A starting point is this observation attributed to Rav:

> The future world is not like this world. In the World to Come there is no eating or drinking, no procreation nor business nor jealousy nor hatred nor competition, but the righteous sit with their crowns on their heads enjoying the radiance of the Divine Presence.   (*Berakhot* 17a)

This passage suggests a very spiritual World to Come. It would appear that the person who pays little attention to mundane emotions and physical satisfaction – perhaps the devoted scholar, the mystic, the ascetic – would be comfortable there. But would the passionate person who enjoys sensory pleasures find this description of the World to Come appealing? Perhaps not, because other texts provide very different, more physical views of the hereafter:

> The Holy One, Blessed be He, will make a great banquet for the righteous on the day he manifests his love for the seed of Isaac [i.e., the end of days].   (*Pesahim* 119b)

> Rava said in the name of R. Yohanan: In the World to Come, the righteous will feast on the flesh of the

> Leviathan and the Holy Blessed One will use its skin to make tabernacles for them. The rest of it will be spread on the walls of Jerusalem. (*Bava Batra* 75a)

> The World to Come is not like this world. In this world there is the trouble of treading and harvesting grapes, but in the World to Come a man will bring one grape on a wagon or a ship, put it in the corner of his house and use [the grape's] contents as if it [were] a wine cask, while its timber [the stalk of the grape] will be used as fire for cooking. (*Ketubbot* 111b)

This is almost the stuff of fairy tales. It would appear that at least some rabbis were prepared to consider a more physical, material World to Come, where, at the end of time, the righteous are rewarded with great banquets or unlimited provisions.

However, some rabbis refuse to speculate about what the World to Come will look like, considering it too mystical a place for humans to invent even in imagination:

> R. Hiya ben Abba also said in the name of R. Yohanan: All our prophets foretell only what will happen in the days of the Messiah, but as for the World to Come, "no eye has seen, O God, besides yours" [Isaiah 64:4]. (*Berakhot* 34b)

By leaving the issue to God in this way, the rabbis are conceding that they cannot unravel the mystery of the World to Come. On the other hand, these rabbis do have a view about "the days of the Messiah" – two views, in fact: a mystical and a more naturalistic view.[16] The quotation above continues, "…and Shmuel disputed this, since he said: 'There is no difference between this world and the days of the Messiah save for Israel's servitude to foreign kingdoms [will be ended].'" This comment provides an earthly view of the messianic era that will precede the World to Come.

Ways to Enter the World to Come

Here and there in the Talmud, the rabbis discuss, as did their predecessors in the Mishnah, who will and will not gain entry to the World to Come. In the Mishnah, most of the discussion is found in chapter 10 of Tractate *Sanhedrin*. In the Talmud, however, the rabbis' comments on the subject appear in many different sections that deal with many different topics. Along the way, the Talmud creates and describes many more routes into the World to Come than were mentioned in the Mishnah.

In the Mishnah the rabbis stressed Torah study as key to attaining the World to Come. The rabbis develop the same idea in the Talmud with some additional insights. For example, in *Ketubbot* 111b, the rabbis record an exchange in which Rabbi Eleazar ben Arakh interprets the verse "The dead will not live" in Isaiah 26:14 to mean that those lax in Torah study will not be resurrected. When Rabbi Yohanan disagrees, Rabbi Eleazar cites Isaiah 26:19 (a text familiar to us as a key text on resurrection): "O, let your dead revive! Let corpses arise: awake and shout for joy, you who dwell in the dust! For your dew is like the dew of light: you make the land of the shades come to life."

Rabbi Eleazar brings the second half of the verse as proof, arguing that "light" refers to Torah. Therefore, the person who makes use of the Torah's light will be revived, but someone who makes no use of it will not. He reads the text to show the Torah's power to secure resurrection – a powerful argument to keep people focused on study.

The Torah is also described as making one's face shine in the World to Come (according to Rabbi Judah in *Sanhedrin* 100a) and as nourishment in the World to Come for a person who starved while alive (according to Rabbi Tanhum in *Sanhedrin* 100a). It would appear, then, that Torah has almost magical curative powers: study will put right all of the wrongs of this life and ensure a person a joyous eternity.

The emphasis on Torah study would seem to leave out women, but Torah and good deeds are required to enter *olam ha-ba*. Women get in on good deeds, as do gentiles; the righteous of the gentiles, we are told, have a share in the World to Come (Tosefta *Sanhedrin* 13).

Some actions which are said to secure entry seem relatively easy to achieve. In *Berakhot* 4b, we are told that if a person follows the *Geulah* prayer directly with the evening *Amidah,* he will secure entry into the World to Come. The same is said of a person who recites *Ashrei* (Psalm 145) three times a day.

It is interesting to note that both of these practices were adopted in the traditional liturgy and indeed remain there today. Were the rabbis trying to draw people into fulfilling the obligation of daily prayer? Offering them so much for relatively little effort would encourage people to pray, thus keeping them engaged in their religious commitments.

Other statements offering the World to Come encourage living in *Eretz Yisrael* (the Land of Israel) as a condition of entry. In *Pesahim* 113a, Rabbi Yohanan is recorded as saying, "Three will inherit the World to Come: he who dwells in *Eretz Yisrael*, he who brings up his sons to study Torah, and he who makes *havdalah* [recites the prayers marking of the end of Sabbath]." Rabbi Jeremiah ben Abba said in the name of Rabbi Yohanan that a person who walks four cubits in the land of Israel merits a share in the World to Come (*Ketubbot* 111a); and on the same page, we find that even a Canaanite bondwoman who lives in the Land of Israel is assured of a place in the World to Come.

There is no category similar to this one in the Mishnah because many of the *tannaim* were living in Israel. By contrast, a few of the *amoraim* were based in the homeland, but many others were living in Babylonia. Consequently, there is an emphasis in the Talmud on bringing people back to *Eretz Yisrael*. The rabbis are once again using the concept of the World to Come to encourage a preferred mode of behavior. We may wonder whether moving to *Eretz Yisrael* from Babylonia had been so difficult at that time that simply doing it would secure someone's place in the World to Come.

Other stories give preference for a share in the World to Come for people engaged in particular occupations. For example:

> R. Berokha used to go often to the market place in Be Lapat, where Elijah often appeared to him. Once, he asked him: Is there anyone in the market who will inherit the World to Come? . . . Two men passed by and Elijah

remarked: These two have a share in the World to Come.
. . . Their occupation? They replied, "We are jesters.
When we see men depressed, we cheer them up. Furthermore, when we see two people quarrelling, we strive hard
to make peace between them." (*Ta'anit* 22a)

The implication here is that through the practice of their profession,
the jesters are contributing to public peace and societal well-being,
another worthy means of gaining access to the World to Come.

There is also a series of legends about a *bat kol* ("daughter of a voice"
or a divine voice) that periodically makes pronouncements from heaven.
Several of these pronouncements relate to particular individuals inherit-
ing the World to Come. For example, in *Avodah Zarah* 18a, the executioner of Rabbi Hanina ben Teradyon, one of the well-known "Ten Martyrs" of the Hadrianic persecutions,[17] asked him during his execution,
"If I help you to a speedier death, will you lead me to the future world?"
The rabbi assented, and the executioner removed the tufts of wet wool
that he had placed over his heart to prolong his agony as he was being
burned to death. A *bat kol* then pronounced that both the rabbi and his
executioner were destined for the World to Come. A similar heavenly
announcement is recorded at the martyrdom of Rabbi Akiva, where the
voice proclaimed: "Happy are you, Rabbi Akiva, that you are ready to
enter the World to Come" (*Berakhot* 61b).

What prompted the rabbis of the Talmud to create so many more
categories for entrance into the World to Come? In contrast to the
categories in the Mishnah, where a degree of hard work, whether study,
spiritual or personal, was required, it seems here that the World to Come
can be attained in a single moment. By dint of a single act, the scales of
the heavenly court can be tipped in an individual's favor. It seems that the
rabbis were eager to expand access to the World to Come, throwing the
gates wide to ensure that as many people as possible could enter.

Perhaps the sages perceived a need during this period (from the third
through the sixth centuries C.E.) for Jews living in exile to feel motivated
and hopeful about their future. The *amoraim* were living a world in which
the depredations of pagan Romans against Judaism and Jews were rapidly

being followed by the antagonism of newly institutionalized Christianity. Even in Sassanid Persia, where Jews suffered much less persecution, they still had to face hardships and discriminatory practices. The Babylonian sages may have held out the promise of the World to Come as a ray of hope in a harsh world.

Other stories in the Talmud suggest more exacting practices that would earn people entry to the World to Come, such as keeping themselves and their children loyal to Torah and Jewish influences:

> When R. Eliezer fell ill, his disciples went in to visit him. They said to him: Master, teach us the paths of life so that we may through them win the life of the World to Come. He said to them: "Be careful of your colleagues' honor, restrain your children from meditation [*higayon*] and sit them between the knees of the sages, and when you pray, know before whom you stand." (*Berakhot* 28b)

It is unclear what is meant by "meditation." One possibility is that it is a warning to keep one's children from studying Greek philosophy, as *higayon* comes from the Hebrew root meaning "logic" or "cogitation." In any case, the passage clearly admonishes Jews to stay with Jewish texts and Jewish prayers before the Hebrew God.

The key word in the above story is respect. In order to obtain a place in the World to Come, one must respect one's colleagues, one's tradition and, above all, one's God. This passage records the deathbed teachings of one of the Talmud's most famous characters, Rabbi Eliezer ben Hyrcanus, who was known for being uncompromising and harsh in his rulings and attitudes. Rabbi Eliezer was excommunicated after a dispute about Jewish law in which he was proved at least partially correct but was overruled by a majority ruling (*Bava Metzia* 59b). He remained embittered, and the Talmud (*Berakhot* 28a) records an alternative version of his death scene in which he laments the fact that his excommunication deprived him from giving, and the world from receiving, the benefit of his enormous learning. In emphasizing to his disciples the importance of respect, he may have been defending the rigor of his own approach to

Jewish law – or alluding to the fact that he felt his own colleagues had treated him disrespectfully.

Another passage teaches that the World to Come is one of the "three precious gifts" that are acquired by suffering:

> Shimon bar Yohai says, "The Holy Blessed One gave Israel three precious gifts. All were given only through suffering. These are the Torah, the land of Israel, and the World to Come." (*Berakhot* 5a)

In contrast to the relative ease of entry to the World to Come through regular prayer and study, Rabbi Shimon bar Yohai tells us that we can only attain the World to Come (and the other benefits of being a Jew) through sacrifice and suffering.

Finally, the rabbis suggest that keeping certain Torah commandments will gain a person entry into the World to Come because the reward for them is explicitly stated in the Torah itself. In *Hullin* 142a, Rabbi Jacob explains a Mishnah that prohibits taking a mother bird with her young in terms of the commandment to honor one's parents. The Torah commands us to "let the mother go, and take only the young [so that the mother bird is spared the pain of seeing her young taken] in order that you may fare well and have a long life" (Deut. 22:7). Rabbi Jacob connects this instruction with the commandment to "honor your father and your mother ... that you may long endure and that you may fare well ...." (Deut. 5:16).

But Rabbi Jacob goes on to ask: What if a person falls to his death while taking a bird's young while letting the mother bird go free? His days are not prolonged! The answer is that his days will be prolonged in "the world which is wholly long" and "wholly good" – that is to say, in the World to Come.

Those Denied Entry to the World to Come

As does the Mishnah, the Talmud identifies categories of people who will not attain the World to Come. Tractate *Sanhedrin* 99a quotes Rabbi Elazar from Mishnah *Avot* 3:15, who listed various violations of Jewish law and ethical commandments as barriers to entrance.

There is a similar behavior-based discussion about why the men of Sodom are denied a portion in the World to Come (Mishnah *Sanhedrin* 10). In *Sanhedrin* 109a, the sages give several reasons for their exclusion based on Genesis 13:13: "The men of Sodom were wicked and sinners before the Lord exceedingly":

- the word "wicked" refers to this world and "sinners" to the World to Come
- they were wicked (that is, immoral) with their bodies and sinners with their money (uncharitable)
- "before the Lord exceedingly" refers to blasphemy and intentional sin

Similarly, the rabbis uphold the exclusion of the generation of the Flood for their arrogance and those who were dispersed after building the Tower of Babel, accusing them of idolatry. However, in discussing groups such as the followers of Korah and the generation of the wilderness, the rabbis introduce some controversy, with several commenting that repentant members of those groups should be admitted to the World to Come. Such discussions, reaching back hundreds of years to biblical personages, indicate how important the sages felt it was to attain the World to Come and reflects the desire some of them had to declare people worthy and allow them to enter, serving as models of repentance.

BODY AND SOUL

The concept that the body and the soul, while different entities, are to be treated as a single unit is an essential component of the talmudic discussion of the hereafter. This is best exemplified by the passage found in *Sanhedrin* 91a–b, attributed to Rabbi Judah ha-Nasi (the codifier of the Mishnah, who is simply called "Rabbi"):[18]

Antoninus said to Rabbi: The body and the soul can both free themselves from judgment. So the body can allege, "The soul has sinned – the proof is that from the day it left me I lie like a dumb stone in the grave and have no power to do anything." The soul can say, "The body has sinned – from the day I left it, I fly through the air like a bird and do not commit any sins."

Rabbi replied: I will tell you a parable. What is this like? A human king who owned a pleasant orchard that contained beautiful fruit. He appointed two watchmen over it, one lame and the other blind. One day the lame man said to the blind, "I can see beautiful fruit in the orchard. Come and put me on your shoulders and we will get it and eat it." So the lame man rode on the blind man's shoulders and they got the fruit and ate it. Some time later, the owner of the orchard came and asked, "Where is that beautiful fruit?" The lame man replied, "What, do I have any feet to walk with?" The blind man replied, "What, do I have eyes to see with?"

What did the owner do? He put the lame man up on the blind man and judged them both together. In the same way, the Holy Blessed One will bring the soul and throw it back into the body and judge them together, as it is written: "He shall call the heavens from above, that He may judge His people" [Ps 50:4]. The heavens are the soul. The earth is the body.

Rabbi clearly sees the soul, represented by the lame man, and the body, represented by the blind man, as a single unit; neither can be successful in gathering the fruit without the other. And they are judged together; the owner of the orchard perceives the relationship that allowed the two men to take the fruit and has them recreate it before judging them. So, too, Rabbi says, will God judge body and soul together.

We can infer from this parable that resurrection as well as final judgment involves both body and soul. First the body rises from the grave.

The soul, which has never perished, then joins the resurrected body, and both stand in judgment before God.

The unity of body and soul is the core concept of the blessing, *Modeh Ani* – rooted in the midrashic text *Genesis Rabbah* (78:1) – that Jews say upon rising every morning:

> I give thanks before You, living and eternal King, who has returned my soul to me with compassion; great is Your faithfulness!

The morning prayer *Elohai neshamah*, found in *Berakhot* 60b, also suggests that by the time of the Talmud, the idea that the body and the soul were separable but functioned as a single unit had gained currency:

> My God, the soul you have given me is pure. You created it, you formed it, you breathed it into me. You guard it within me, and you are destined to take it from me and return it to me in the future to come ....

While the soul, in these blessings, is seen as separable from the body (since it can be removed from and put back into the body), this does not denote a dualistic approach to body and soul. Unlike the Greeks, who believed that the soul was a noble creature reluctantly imprisoned in the gross body, the talmudic sages believed that the soul and the body, though separate entities, were inextricably bound to each other.

Does this imply that the rabbis believed in immortality of the soul? The texts noted above suggest that they do. They portray a body that initially dies but a soul that is simply removed from the body when the body dies. The soul goes up to heaven or *Gan Eden* and takes residence there with other souls to wait until the end of days, when the Messiah comes and resurrection will take place. At that point, the body and soul are reunited.

As for the condition of those who are to enjoy resurrection, there is also some speculation about the state in which the dead will arise. If there is to be actual physical resurrection, what shape will bodies be in?

It is concluded that bodies are resurrected in the state in which they died, though it is possible for healing to take place after that. For example, a person identified as Queen Cleopatra[19] asks Rabbi Meir whether the dead will be naked or clothed. Rabbi Meir answers that in the same way that wheat rises "clothed" [in its outer covering, the chaff], so will the dead (*Sanhedrin* 90b). Similarly, Resh Lakish and Rava both allege that people will be revived with the defects they had when they died, but will subsequently be healed (*Sanhedrin* 91b).

One of the most moving passages about death and dying occurs at the end of Tractate *Mo'ed Katan*:

> Rava, while seated at the bedside of R. Nahman, saw him sinking into slumber [death]. He said to Rava, "Tell him, Sir, not to torment me" [referring to the Angel of Death]. Rava said, "Are you, Sir, not a man esteemed?" R. Nahman replied, "Who is esteemed, who is regarded, who is distinguished [before the Angel of Death]?"
>
> Rava said, "Do, Sir, show yourself to me [in a dream]." He did show himself. Rava asked him, "Did you suffer pain, Sir?" R. Nahman replied, "As [little as] taking a hair out of milk. If the Holy One, Blessed be He, were to ask me to go back to the world as I was, I would not want to, because the fear of death is so great."
>
> (*Mo'ed Katan* 28a)[20]

This passage reminds us that the rabbis are also human beings with their own mortal fears. Rava, sitting at the deathbed of Rabbi Nahman, sees his friend's terror of dying and asks him to let him know in a dream what the other side is like when he gets there. The message seems to be that death can be gentle and is not to be feared.

5

Medieval Jewish Philosophy: Faith and Reason

W HAT IS THE soul? Can the soul survive apart from the body? What part of a person's essence survives in the World to Come? These questions, posed by medieval Jewish philosophers, sound like questions we might ask today, though framed in another historical context with its own issues and concerns. From the tenth to the fifteenth centuries, Jewish thinkers tried to reconcile Jewish beliefs with the demands of reason, science, and philosophy, as well as defend Judaism against the competing claims of other faiths. Although their works seldom focused exclusively on the afterlife, all the thinkers we will discuss dealt with this subject in the context of their total approach to Judaism.

The Jewish scholars who had the most immediate impact on Jewish thought in this period lived in the Islamic world: Muslim Spain, Egypt, and other countries around the Mediterranean. These thinkers were influenced by the surrounding Arabic cultures; indeed, most of the important Jewish works from this period were written in Arabic and translated later into Hebrew. Moreover, they were able to read the writings of the ancient Greek philosophers in Arabic translations.

It was during this period that the two major cultures within world Jewry became distinct: the *Ashkenazim* of Central and Western Europe and the *Sephardim* of Spain and the Middle East. While the Ashkenazic world of the Middle Ages produced great thinkers – premier among them Rabbenu Gershom Me'or ha-Golah (ca. 960–1028) and Rabbi Shlomo ben Yitzhak, known as Rashi (1040–1105) – their scholarship was shaped differently from that of the Mediterranean Jewish scholars. The Ashkenazic sages tended to continue the traditions of talmudic text-based learning, delving deeply into the received tradition. They did so largely in isolation from their Christian neighbors and did not engage in religious dialogue with them unless challenged to debate by Christian leaders. Their discussions of the afterlife in their commentaries on the Bible and the Talmud tended to be passing references that affirmed the concepts of bodily resurrection and the World to Come, but they did not produce full monographs or sections of major works on these subjects.

The Sephardic thinkers of this period were generally considered to be more worldly. They lived in the "Golden Age" of Arabic culture, when Muslims were making strides in mathematics, science, literature and philosophy, and Jews who lived and worked alongside them were exposed to Arabic thought and culture. Sephardic Jews were also better off economically than their Ashkenazic counterparts, which afforded them greater mobility and interaction with people of other cultures. Consequently, the works of the Sephardic scholars look beyond the received tradition to the ideas of others. They had unprecedented access both to classical philosophical texts through Arabic translations and to contemporary philosophy and scientific discussion. These elements help make the writings of these sages seem forward-looking and even relevant to modern readers, although the abstract nature of their concepts and the elevated language make their works difficult to understand.

The most influential Sephardic thinkers of this period were caught up in the perceived conflict between religion and philosophy and although they are commonly referred to as Jewish medieval philosophers, their works are basically theological in subject and intention. They sought to prove that Judaism could hold its own as a source of truth in a world that also contains scientific and philosophical realities. At this time, representatives of Islam and Christianity frequently asserted the supremacy of their faiths and challenged Jews to demonstrate the validity of Judaism as a belief system. Accordingly, Jewish thinkers of the period attempted to clarify Judaism's position in relation to other religions in much greater detail than the rabbis of the Talmud. When the talmudic sages spoke of people who practiced other religions, it was more often than not simply to warn Jews to associate with them as little as possible so that they would not be tainted by their beliefs.

The medieval Jewish thinkers, unlike the rabbis of the Talmud, also tried to deal with subjects systematically. While the Talmud deals only sporadically with the idea of the soul's immortality, the philosophers of the Middle Ages give the subject their full attention, examining and discussing it thoroughly, often enumerating and analyzing arguments for and against a particular point before coming to a conclusion.These medieval thinkers had great respect for the human intellect. Repeatedly we see them extolling the virtues of rational thought and analysis. Developing the intellect seemed to them almost a sacred duty. They also regarded intellectual development as a way of attaining communion with God. This concept influenced their views on the nature of the soul as well.

Some of the subject matter and ideas put forward by the Sephardic scholars of the Middle Ages will seem very esoteric, even cryptic, to us. We should bear in mind that what they considered scientific fact was much less sophisticated and complete than what we know today. They believed, for example, that every object in the universe was composed of a combination of the "four elements" – earth, water, fire, and air – an idea, of course, that has been superseded.

To set the context for this discussion, let us take look at some of the ideas about the soul that were in circulation at the time. A philosopher was likely to identify with one of two schools of classical Greek thought: neo-Platonic (based on the ideas of Plato, c. 427–347 B.C.E., as reinterpreted by medieval thinkers) or Aristotelian (based on the philosophy of Aristotle, 384–322 B.C.E.). In the neo-Platonic system, the soul is considered to be an element from a higher world residing in the body, having arrived there through a process of emanation from the One, an incomprehensible and absolute unity. Thus the soul is a pale reflection of the perfection of the place from which it came.

Thinkers who based their philosophy on Aristotle saw the soul as the first "actuality" of a body – the animating force that made it a living thing and not just matter. He listed three different kinds of souls: those for plants, animals, and humans. Only human beings possess souls that are rational, in that they have the ability to reason theoretically. Aristotle saw the soul as connected to the body and inseparable from it; neither could exist independently. At the same time, he regarded that aspect of mind or intellect associated with the soul to be connected with the "Active Intellect" in the universe. Aristotelian thinkers believed that this connection gave the human soul a measure of immortality.

The Jewish philosophers drew on elements from both systems, reframing their arguments in a specifically Jewish context. They too discuss the nature of the soul at considerable length, but for our purposes, we will limit ourselves to their ideas about what happens to the soul in the hereafter.

SA'ADIAH GAON

What is the nature of the soul and is the soul immortal? This question was taken up by Sa'adiah ben Yosef (Sa'adiah Gaon, 882–942 C.E.), who is considered the foremost early medieval Jewish thinker. A renowned legal scholar, Sa'adiah rose to become the head (*gaon*) of the rabbinic academy in Pumbedita, Babylonia. He also produced Judaism's first philosophical treatise, known as *Sefer ha-Emunot ve-ha-De'ot* ("The Book of Beliefs and Opinions").[1] Sa'adiah places great importance on the human intellect, which he sees as one of the primary instruments for the revelation of truth to humankind, the other two being Torah and the Oral Law. It is significant that he champions *both* human reason and revelation as valid sources of knowledge.

Sa'adiah believed that Judaism could hold its own against challenges from other religions as well as from philosophy and science. He also sought to refute specific views held by other faiths: Christians, whose doctrines of Jesus as Messiah and a Trinitarian God were well established by the ninth century; Zoroastrians, whose beliefs included what Sa'adiah saw as dual Creators, as opposed to the Jewish concept of a single, omnipotent God; and those he perceived as heretics among his own people, particularly the Karaites, who accepted the written Torah but denied rabbinic authority. Sa'adiah's book stands as a reasoned defense of basic Jewish beliefs for Jews in his times. Without Sa'adiah, Maimonides observes over two hundred years later, Torah would have disappeared.

Among the many topics that Sa'adiah treats in his major work, he endeavors to explain the nature of the soul, which he calls by the Hebrew word, *nefesh*. In the sixth treatise of *Sefer ha-Emunot ve-ha-De'ot*, he rejects a number of "scientific" theories that tie the composition of the soul to the natural elements of air and fire, to something in the blood, to a juncture of the senses, or to any other aspect of nature or human physiology. Instead, he presents the theory that the soul is created by God, but not as part of the body; rather, it is embedded in the heart at the time that the body is created. His description of the soul emphasizes its fineness in comparison with other creations:

> As for the quality of its substance, it is comparable in purity as that of the heavenly spheres. Like the latter, it attains luminosity as a result of the light that it receives from God, except that its substance becomes, in consequence thereof, even finer than that of the spheres. That is how it came to be endowed with the power of speech.[2]

Why would God put this fine soul into the crude body? Sa'adiah responds with an analogy: although the soul is not made of fire, it is like fire, which cannot exist unless it is attached to something else. Hence the soul can serve God only if it is attached to the body. Heart and soul remain united for "a period," ostensibly the person's lifetime, and then God separates heart and soul again. How does this happen? When a person dies, Sa'adiah speculates, an angel dispatched by God appears to him in the form of a figure of yellowish fire with eyes of blue fire. The dying person shudders, and God separates his soul from his body.

God stores the souls until the time of retribution, or the end of days. Pure souls are kept on high and turbid or troubled ones are sent down below. When a requisite number of souls are gathered (Sa'adiah doesn't tell us how many), and the Messiah proclaims that the end of the world is at hand, God will resurrect the righteous and punish the wicked, reuniting the souls and bodies of the righteous in the World to Come and sending the undeserving to the underworld.

In his defense of Jewish eschatology, Sa'adiah is clear that there will be bodily resurrection. He gives four proofs for this belief, drawn from nature, reason, Scripture, and tradition, and states repeatedly that resurrection is an "approved idea" that every Jew should adopt. In Sa'adiah's view, every righteous and penitent Jew will be resurrected. Family members will recognize each other, and the resurrected people will eat, drink, and marry, though subsequently in the World to Come they will no longer need the bodily functions of eating and drinking and will survive without them, as Moses did on Sinai.

It is vital for Jews to believe in resurrection, he maintains, enumerating the benefits of this belief, among them: that will help people believe in God's omnipotence; that families will be reunited; and that once the dead have come back to life, they will be able to explain what death was like and how they came to be resurrected, thus satisfying our curiosity. Speaking more personally, he adds: "It is my ardent wish I might be among those who will witness [the resurrection] either in my own lifetime or by being resurrected as a reward for my contribution to the welfare of my people."[3]

JUDAH HALEVI

In contrast to the other medieval philosophers, Judah Halevi's mission was not to reconcile Judaism with philosophy. Despite his great respect for Aristotelian philosophy, he felt that any philosophy based on human reasoning fell short when compared with the revelation upon which Judaism is based. According to Halevi, the Bible is rational, but its truth is superior to anything that can be attained by the use of human reason alone.

Judah Halevi (before 1075–1141), born in southern Spain (the specific city is a matter of dispute), is known primarily as a Hebrew poet, but he was also a physician and a philosopher. Although he traveled widely during his lifetime, he may never have fulfilled his ambition to immigrate to the Land of Israel and probably died in Egypt – although, according to legend, he did reach Jerusalem only to be trampled to death by a horse.

Halevi's philosophy is contained in a single work, "The Book of Argument and Proof in Defense of the Despised Religion." Written in Arabic and translated into Hebrew, it is more commonly known as *The Kuzari* after the Khazars, a Turkic tribe that flourished in what is now Russia from the seventh to tenth centuries. It was believed, possibly with some basis in fact, that around the year 740, the Khazars converted to Judaism *en masse* at the instigation of their king.

The Kuzari is a polemic written primarily in dialogue form with a Jewish protagonist as the spokesman for Halevi's views. It begins with the portrayal of the king of the Khazars being told in a dream that his deeds are not what God expects of him. The troubled king consults a philosopher, a Christian, and a Muslim to address this issue. Unsatisfied with their answers, he then consults a Jew, whose arguments in favor of Judaism he finds persuasive. *The Kuzari* contains relatively few references to the hereafter, but those arguments help to persuade the king of the superiority of Judaism over philosophy and other religious faiths.

In Halevi's view, the Jews have a unique affinity for prophecy – hearing and experiencing the word of God. Central to his argument is the premise that knowledge that comes from the experience of prophecy is more trustworthy than that which comes from abstract philosophical systems. Jews experienced the revelation at Sinai, which imparted to them knowledge of the actions and deeds that God required of them. The teachings of the other two faiths, he argues, are pale reflections of this pivotal event.

The Jewish protagonist in *The Kuzari* proposes that a person who comes into contact with a prophet experiences "a spiritual renewal when he hears the divine words," which causes his soul to aspire to new levels of humility and purity. This experience, for him, provides proof of the independent existence of the soul and of the soul's immortality:

> When you find a set of teachings that contains wisdom
> and practices that bring the individual to such a lofty

state (when the teachings are utilized in the designated
place and performed using the designated methods) this
set of teachings will undoubtedly also preserve the soul
after the body has passed away.[4]

Thus the knowledge imparted through prophecy gives the soul eventual access to the divine realm. It also proves the existence of a World to Come, Halevi writes, since the soul of the person enlightened by the prophet will want to separate from the body and enter the divine realm. The fact that it is imprisoned in the body means that it must wait until after death to reunite with its divine source, at which point it becomes immortal. Then the soul will be able to see the divine radiance of the spiritual world and hear the voice of God, just as the prophets did when they received their visions.

Because Halevi viewed prophecy as unique to Judaism, he argued that only Judaism could promise immortality of the soul and life in the World to Come. He has nothing to add to the discussions of *Gan Eden* and *Gehinnom* in the Talmud except to say that these are a comprehensive treatment of the subject and nothing more is required.

Although Halevi believes that only Judaism can offer immortality, he concedes that there is little in the Bible itself about life after death. Still he is able to point out verses in the prophetic books that talk about the return of the human body to the earth and the spirit returning to God, such as Ecclesiastes 12:7: "And the dust returns to the earth as it was, and the spirit returns to God, Who gave it." He cites Daniel 12:2 and observes that both Elijah and Enoch were "taken" by God without actually dying. And he alludes to the episode of the Witch of Endor (I Samuel 28), in which Saul speaks to his dead mentor, Samuel, to prove that those who lived in the time of the prophets believed in the immortality of the soul.

Later in the work, the Jew tells the king in some detail about the arguments of Aristotelian philosophers. For example, they teach that the soul controls the faculty of imagination in a human being, that it functions as the seat of wisdom, and that it is distinct from the body in that it does not age, nor is it weakened by use.[5] When the king expresses approval of these ideas, the Jew argues that the king runs the risk of being seduced and points out a critical difference between Judaism and philosophy: the philosophers' theories about metaphysics are not proven. They are mere conjectures, while Judaism bases itself on the experience of revelation:

> Once you have accepted the premise that the universe . . . came into existence by God's will . . . you will no longer need to trouble yourself with the questions of how physical bodies came to exist and how souls integrate with them . . . . You will also be able to accept . . . the stories that describe what we may expect for the messianic era, the resurrection of the dead and the World to Come. Our correct and accepted traditional account has already verified the soul's survival, regardless of any argument as to whether the soul is physical or purely spiritual.

Halevi clearly has no interest in splitting hairs over these issues. His approach, based on faith, is theological rather than philosophical. While he is knowledgeable about current philosophical ideas he considers them unequal to the task of explaining an unknown like the afterlife. In the end, Halevi argues that revelation, direct religious experience, trumps philosophy.

א   MOSES MAIMONIDES

What part of a person survives in the World to Come – body, soul, or intellect? Is the next world a physical or spiritual place? Followers of the classical Greek philosophers had a spiritualized notion of the individual intellect rejoining its original source, while the rabbinical imagination held on to the belief in both bodily resurrection and the soul's immortality. Maimonides, as the leading rabbi of his day and a scholar well versed in Aristotelian philosophy, negotiated a position between the two belief systems. But the subject of the hereafter was an area of tension for him, and despite his ingenious solution members of the Jewish community challenged him repeatedly to clarify and defend his views.

Known in the Jewish world as Rambam, an acronym for the initials of his Hebrew name, Moses ben Maimon, Maimonides (1135–1204) is considered the greatest of the medieval Jewish rabbinic scholars, codifiers, and philosophers; his tombstone bears the epitaph "From Moses [the Prophet] to Moses [Maimonides] there was no one like Moses." He was also a physician and advisor to heads of state; in other words, a religious man who was at home in the secular world.

Born in Córdoba, Spain, Maimonides fled with his family to Morocco when he was thirteen, after Córdoba fell to the Almohad Muslims, a fanatical dynasty that persecuted Jews. After that, he lived in Palestine and Egypt, where he became the physician of the sultan, Saladin. His main works are his *Commentary on the Mishnah* (1158–1168), the *Mishneh Torah* (1180), a comprehensive code of Jewish law, and *Guide to the Perplexed* (1190). These are only his major works: Maimonides, a prolific author, wrote many responsa (written answers to questions about Jewish law), essays on Jewish law, and medical treatises. He used Arabic for all his writing except the *Mishneh Torah*, which he wrote in Hebrew.

Maimonides first deals with the subject of the hereafter in his *Commentary on the Mishnah*. Motivated perhaps by a desire to educate a populace he saw as superstitious and ill-informed, he states that the aim of his book is to resolve and clarify Jewish teachings about the afterlife. Commenting on the passage from *Sanhedrin* 10, he sets out his views on the soul:

> Just as a blind man cannot conceive of color, nor a deaf person of sound, nor a eunuch of the desire for sex, so, too, the body cannot appreciate the pleasure of the soul. Just as fish do not know the element of fire – for they live in the midst of its very opposite – so, too, it is impossible to appreciate spiritual pleasure in this physical world.[6]

This view of the spiritually evolved and sophisticated soul informs Maimonides' perception of the World to Come, which he then describes:

> [In] the spiritual world, which is the World to Come, our souls will be informed by the knowledge of the Creator,

may He be blessed, in the manner in which the heavenly bodies are informed of Him, or even more . . . . Our sages said: "The righteous sit with their crowns on their heads enjoying the radiance of the Divine Presence." The intent behind the words "crowns on their heads" is to convey the immortality of the soul by virtue of its intellectual continuity, which is identical with the Deity.

He goes on to explain that those souls who enjoy God's presence will do so in the same way as angels and other holy beings do, in a completely spiritual way. The ultimate aspiration of humans is therefore to attain this level of knowledge of God, in order to merit this glory after death. Citing "earlier philosophers" (referring to Aristotle), he maintains that the existence of the soul parallels the existence of God, as both are eternal; just as God brought the world into being, the soul brings ideas into being. Conversely, the punishment for a wicked life is a soul that is cut off from others and does not endure after the body's death.[7]

For Maimonides, the World to Come is based on spiritual and intellectual perfection. Clearly, he believes in the soul's immortality. It is notable that no Jewish thinker prior to Maimonides expressed this concept as explicitly as he does. His prooftext seems to be the statement of Rav from the Talmud, which completely spiritualizes the World to Come: "In the World to Come there is no eating or drinking, no procreation nor business nor jealousy nor hatred nor competition, but the righteous sit with their crowns on their heads enjoying the radiance of the Divine Presence" (*Berakhot* 17a), although he does not quote it verbatim.

If there are no physical functions in the World to Come, it would appear that bodies are not necessary either. This raises the question: where does bodily resurrection – which, as we have seen, is a central tenet of rabbinic Judaism – fit into the scheme? Even Maimonides has difficulty reconciling the two concepts.

In contrast to the care he takes in explicating the World to Come, Maimonides treats the subject of resurrection as an axiom. He simply states:

> The resurrection of the dead is one of the fundamental principles taught by Moses. A person who does not believe this has no faith, nor does he share any bond with Judaism.[8]

Maimonides' dilemma is clear: he is faced with what seems to be a direct conflict of ideas. On the one hand, there is a doctrine that mandates belief in an actual physical resurrection. On the other hand, he regards the soul as elevated, rational, immortal. So how can a revivified body fit in with the spiritual conditions of the World to Come?

At the end of his commentary on Tractate *Sanhedrin,* Maimonides expounds his so-called "Thirteen Principles."[9] These, he states, are the essential beliefs of the sacred Torah. Belief in these concepts is the cornerstone of Jewish identity, and disputing any one of them is the mark of a heretic.

The Thirteen Principles include belief in resurrection, though the list does not mention belief in the World to Come. Again Maimonides is extremely brief: in contrast to his treatment of all the other principles, he deals with resurrection in a single sentence: "The thirteenth fundamental principle is the resurrection of the dead, which we have already explained." Yet he did not explain it elsewhere; he simply stated earlier that resurrection is a fundamental principle of Jewish tradition.

In subsequent works, Maimonides continues to be occupied with the subject of the hereafter. In the section of *Mishneh Torah* that describes the "Laws of Repentance" (*Hilkhot Teshuvah*), he once again states his position about the World to Come:

> In the World to Come there is no body or physical form, only the souls of the righteous alone, without a body, like the ministering angels .... Consequently the statement "the righteous sit" [from *Berakhot* 17a] must be interpreted metaphorically. Similarly, the phrase "their crowns on their heads": [this is] the knowledge that they grasped, which will allow them to merit the life of the World to Come.[10]

Elsewhere in the same work he is dismissive of bodies and their appetites, stating: "In a situation where there is no body, all of these matters will be nullified." Once again, we can see that his conception of the World to Come is entirely spiritual and noncorporeal. He also suggests that since death is a physical phenomenon, souls will not suffer it; souls will live on eternally in the World to Come, he affirms in a firm and unequivocal statement of belief in the soul's immortality.

Yet resurrection is never mentioned in the discussion of the *Hilkhot Teshuvah*. How can this be? Maimonides himself had previously stated that resurrection is a fundamental belief of the Jewish faith, yet it is missing in this discussion. Perhaps this reflects a continuing tension between the mandated belief in the resurrection of the physical, earthbound body and his more passionate devotion to the spiritual, intellectual realm of the soul.

As a result of this omission, Maimonides became embroiled in a controversy concerning his views on resurrection. An academy student in Damascus declared that, based on Maimonides' writings, he no longer believed in bodily resurrection. Maimonides dismissed the incident as a misunderstanding, but the subject surfaced again in 1189 when a writer from Yemen said that many Yemenite Jews were denying the principle of resurrection, in part because of his writings, and asked for a responsum. Maimonides wrote back affirming his faith in resurrection as a basic creed, but he was subsequently attacked by the head of the Baghdad Academy on the same issue. In order to put the matter to rest, Maimonides wrote *Ma'amar tehiyat ha-metim* ("Essay on the Resurrection of the Dead") around 1191.[11]

Maimonides begins the essay by referring to the reports from Damascus, Yemen, and Baghdad that accuse him of denying the doctrine of resurrection. Clearly annoyed that he must state his position again, Maimonides writes:

> Let the discerning student know that our intent in this treatise is to explain that in which we believe relating to this fundamental principle concerning which controversy arose among the scholars . . . . This treatise contains

nothing new or additional to that which we have already
said . . . .[12]

But Maimonides does bring in something new. Here he confirms
that resurrection is a fundamental creed in Judaism, citing Daniel 12:2
and Daniel 12:13 ("But you, go on to the end: you shall rest and rise in
your destiny at the end of the days") in support. Moreover, he argues
that bodily resurrection must be taken literally and angrily alleges that he
never said it could be interpreted as anything else or viewed as metaphor.
He then goes on to explain that once the soul has been returned to the
body, the revived individuals will live full lives, including eating, drinking, and having children. He says that they will live extremely long lives
like those of the days of the Messiah, but they will then die once more:

> Further, the life following which there is no death is the
> life in the World to Come, because there are no [physi-
> cal] bodies there. We firmly believe – and this is the truth
> that every intelligent person accepts – that in the World
> to Come souls without bodies will exist like angels.[13]

This concept of a "double dying,"[14] which is entirely new, enables
Maimonides to sustain his carefully considered ideal of a spiritual World
to Come, but still affirm the doctrine of bodily resurrection. His final
position seems to be that one must still believe in resurrection in order
to achieve immortality. Resurrection is a miracle that the book of Daniel
predicted. Physical resurrection will actually take place at some stage,
with souls returning to bodies. However, humans should ultimately
aspire to improve themselves on earth, so that their souls would subsequently attain the spiritual perfection of the World to Come. There the
pure, evolved soul will find everlasting enjoyment in the Divine Presence
with no physical body to impede this process.

The impression with which he leaves us is the one we may have
formed originally: that Maimonides concerned himself more with the
spiritual concept of the soul's immortality than with the Scripturally
"factual" idea of physical resurrection. This may be in part because for

him, bodily resurrection was a given, an irrefutable cornerstone of Judaism, a miracle he refused to deny. In his personal philosophy, however, he clearly exalted the spiritual over the physical.

Why did Maimonides choose to include the belief in resurrection as a basic principle in his Thirteen Principles without mention of the World to Come (and therefore of the immortality of the soul)? He might have considered that the masses, to whom the Thirteen Principles were directed, were not in a position to understand the lofty nature of the World to Come as he conceived it. He himself may have viewed the soul and the intellect so purely in terms of spirit without physical substance that no world was necessary to house them. From his metaphorical interpretation of *Berakhot* 17a discussed above, it is evident that Maimonides saw the World to Come not as the home for resurrected persons but as a place for disembodied immortal souls. But here he affirms only that a belief in resurrection is essential to Judaism.

Maimonides, the Jewish sage as well as the rationalist philosopher, clearly regarded this tenet of Jewish belief as paramount in this context. Perhaps he recognized its importance to the community and to Jewish law, or he felt it was necessary to inspire the kind of behavior that would merit immortality. In either case, the controversy over his teachings about the hereafter continued to rage both during his lifetime and after his death.

NAHMANIDES

Does the soul's journey continue after death? Where does it stay until the end of days? If Maimonides saw the World to Come as a purely spiritual realm and *Gan Eden* and *Gehinnom* as metaphors rather than actual places, then Nahmanides, the other rabbinical giant of this period, wanted to know more about the "world of souls" at various stages of judgment. He brings to the conversation the rigor of a philosopher and the erudition of a talmudist combined with the imagination of a mystic. His work occupies the middle ground between philosophy and mysticism.

Rabbi Moses ben Nahman (1194–1270), known also as Nahmanides and by the acronym Ramban, was a thirteenth-century Spanish talmudist, kabbalist, and biblical commentator. As a spiritual leader of thirteenth-century Spanish Jewry, Nahmanides mediated disputes between factions within the Jewish community and represented Judaism in disputations when called upon to do so by the Christian rulers. In 1263, he received an award from the king after an impressive performance in the Disputation of Barcelona against a Jewish-born apostate, Pablo Christiani. Nevertheless, he had to flee his homeland because of threats from the Dominican priests backed by the pope. Settling in Palestine in old age, he lived first in Jerusalem, then in Acre. Perhaps it was his immigration to Palestine that informed his pronouncements that the resettlement of the land of Israel (*yishuv Eretz Yisrael*) was a biblical precept. He is the first of the prominent medieval commentators to do so.

Considered normative and even conservative in his extensive writings on Jewish law, he is also the first commentator to use insights from Kabbalah, the Jewish mystical tradition, in his Bible commentaries. Nahmanides is more open than his predecessors to esoteric ideas and less invested in trying to provide rational proofs and explanations for faith-based phenomena. For example, while Maimonides considers the possibility that the angels who visited Abraham in Genesis 18 were a vision, Nahmanides insists that they were indeed angels.

His discussion of the hereafter is set in a moral framework relating to reward and punishment, a central theme in his work. The problem of theodicy – why the innocent suffer and evil seemingly goes unpunished – weighs heavily upon him. In his commentary on the book of Job, he even suggests that suffering may be atonement for the sins of a past life. The concept of *gilgul,* the transmigration of souls, is an idea borrowed from early kabbalistic literature. While Sa'adiah and Joseph Albo (whose philosophy we will discuss later in this chapter) reject the notion of *gilgul* outright and Maimonides and Halevi make no mention of it, Nahmanides is willing to consider the possibility of transmigration and reincarnation.

Nahmanides' main ideas about the hereafter may be found in his work entitled *Sha'ar ha-Gemul* ("Gate of Reward"). It was first published in Naples in 1490 and later incorporated into his larger treatise, *Torat ha-Adam* ("Law of Man"), a detailed study of Jewish law relating to death and mourning. In *Gate of Reward,* Nahmanides presents a system for what happens after death, grounding his ideas in earlier rabbinic tradition, which gives some elements of his schema a basis in the Talmud. He begins with the statement that humans are judged during their lifetimes, especially at Rosh ha-Shanah, again immediately after their death, and finally before they enter the World to Come. It is part of Nahmanides' thesis that if people suffer in this lifetime, that suffering is most likely to be punishment for wrongs they might have committed. However, not all wrongs are punished in this lifetime. Some are punished after death.

Immediately after death, according to Nahmanides, the individual is judged and assigned to one of three categories. Those who were thoroughly righteous in their lifetimes are inscribed and sealed for life in the World to Come, then dispatched to *Gan Eden.* Those who were thoroughly wicked, who were heretics, or who caused others to sin are sent straight to *Gehinnom.* The "intermediate" ones (*benonim*), who were neither particularly righteous nor particularly wicked, "cry out for a place of tranquillity."[15] They are judged generously, but those found to have been more wicked than good also go to *Gehinnom.* Their punishment depends on how badly they behaved and is proportionate to their wickedness.

A final judgment will take place at each person's destination. At that point, the souls in *Gan Eden* go to the World to Come, as do the souls that have been punished sufficiently in *Gehinnom* for the wrongs they committed during their lifetimes. A worse fate awaits the wicked.

Nahmanides describes in some detail what both *Gehinnom* and *Gan Eden* will be like by knitting together various *midrashim.* The difference between his discussion and that of the rabbis of the Talmud and the Midrash upon which he bases his ideas is that his version is more systematic and sits within a coherent moral/psychological context of reward and punishment.

Gehinnom

Unlike Maimonides, Nahmanides presents *Gehinnom* as an actual place, with punishment directed against bodies as well as souls. In fact, he is remarkably specific about what *Gehinnom* is like; drawing on scattered references in the Talmud and various *midrashim,* he creates a mosaic of ideas and images that form a recognizable picture.

After discussing the size of *Gehinnom* (sixty times the size of *Gan Eden,* which itself is sixty times bigger than the world) and its various entrances on earth, he describes its seven levels: *Gehenna,* the gates of the shadow of death, the gates of death, the slimy clay, the pit of ruin, destruction, and Sheol.[16] These, he suggests, correspond to various types of wickedness.[17] The lowest level, *Arka,* is where angels of destruction place the wicked under a river of fire that comes from beneath the throne of glory:

> No one who admits the creation of the soul by His will, blessed be He, will deny that it is possible [for God] to create an ethereal opposite matter that would be the counterpart [of the soul and able] to destroy it. Indeed, our rabbis of blessed memory say of the very angels that they are burnt in the River of Fire, and they also mention "fire devouring fire."[18]

In *Gehinnom,* the souls of sinners are punished with suffering and pain that have no parallel in this world:

> This is because suffering in this world affects the lowly body, which is bulky in creation and slow in sensitivity, while the grave punishment and pain affect the soul, which is pure and refined in its creation. This is analogous to a person experiencing greater sensitivity, when a needle touches his flesh, than an ass would experience in a similar situation . . . . There is no comparison or likeness whatsoever between the extremely great suffering of the soul and the bodily pain of living creatures.[19]

There are three options for the souls of the wicked with regard to this pain. The first is that their suffering will expiate their wrongs.

Nahmanides gives the example of a person who was otherwise religious but could not resist eating forbidden fat. Such a person will still be able to gain entry into the World to Come at the final judgment. The other two possibilities, for people who were more wicked than that in their lifetimes, relate to the "excision" of the soul, which Nahmanides says, "in truth is the destruction of the soul."[20]

Many Jewish commentators on the hereafter have discussed the excision of the soul. Like the rabbis of the Talmud, they cite Numbers 15:31:

> Because he has scorned the word of the Lord and breached his commandment, that soul shall be cut off – yes, cut off [hikaret tikaret]: he bears his guilt.

The amoraim read the repetition of "cut off" as referring to losing one's life both in this world and in the World to Come. Maimonides, following similar reasoning, understands the verse to refer to the ultimate punishment: that the disembodied soul will be cut off and not endure.

Nahmanides develops this view even further. In his vision of Gehinnom, there are two versions of excision. The first is that after twelve months, the soul of a wicked person is burned away by the heavenly fire mentioned above and its ashes are scattered under the feet of the righteous. At that point, the soul's suffering ceases: it is not punished further. The irretrievably wicked, however, remain in Gehinnom forever, constantly suffering and permanently denied any relief. Naturally, they are also denied entry to the World to Come.

Gan Eden

Gan Eden is the complete opposite of Gehinnom. This is where the righteous are sent when they die, pending the final judgment. Nahmanides is once again very specific about what it is like. He draws together elements from Tanakh, Talmud, and midrashim to show that it is located on this earth and that four rivers emerge from it (one of which surrounds the land of Israel). Nahmanides alleges that travelers' accounts of having seen the flaming sword (mentioned in Genesis 3:24 as having been placed at the entrance to *Gan Eden* to bar Eve and Adam from returning there) are true.

However, *Gan Eden* also has a mystical dimension, containing clues that only people skilled in mysticism are capable of reading. For Nahmanides, *Gan Eden* is God's laboratory for designing souls:

> The first man, the handiwork of the Holy One, blessed be He, was the epitome of mankind in understanding and knowledge, and God, blessed be He, set him in the best of places for bodily enjoyment and benefit. In that honored place He designed the entire function of the higher world, the World of Souls . . . .[21]

Nahmanides is describing the place where God designed the whole upper world, including all forms of creation – physical, spiritual, and angelic. *Gan Eden* is the most honored of locations in the lower world because the centers of the middle and upper worlds are located over it. Therefore, more visions of God are seen in *Gan Eden* than anywhere else in the world. The souls of those who dwell there become elevated by studying the higher secrets and by experiencing visions of God in the company of the higher beings of that place. Nahmanides' vision of this world of souls anticipates the English poet John Keats' characterization of the world not as a vale of tears, but as "a vale of soul-making."[22]

Gan Eden is a training ground where the soul learns about how to cleave to the higher world and how to enjoy spiritual pleasure. Souls converse with each other by way of knowledge and perception. Nahmanides uses the terms *Gan Eden* and "the world of souls" interchangeably to refer to the place where the righteous enjoy their rewards after death. However, he draws a clear distinction between these places and the World to Come after resurrection.

The World to Come

As mentioned above, Nahmanides suggests that all souls will be subject to a final judgment. He places this event at the end of the Messianic era:

At the conclusion thereof [of the Messianic era] the judgment and the resurrection of the dead will occur. This is the recompense which includes the body and the soul. This is the great principle which is the hope of all who look longingly to the Holy One, Blessed be He. It is the World to Come, in which the body will become like the soul and the soul will cleave to the knowledge of the Most High, just as it adhered to it in *Gan Eden* and the World of Souls. Now, however, it will be elevated to an even greater degree of perception than heretofore, and the existence of all will be forever and ever.[23]

So for Nahmanides, there is actual physical resurrection. He states that the World to Come will indeed be physical – its inhabitants will have bodies; they will gather in the Sanctuary; the Sanctuary will display its vessels. It is striking that in his system, the soul and the body have become interdependent once more, as in the story from the Talmud of the lame man and the blind man (*Sanhedrin* 91a); he also uses as a prooftext Elijah's ascent to heaven, in which his body and soul remained intact. In this respect, Nahmanides differs noticeably from Maimonides, who describes the World to Come as purely spiritual World to Come.

Nahmanides also deals with Rav's text from the Talmud about the resurrected beings, the righteous who merit the World to Come, being nourished by the light of the *Shekhinah*. He reads this as a reference to the resurrected beings obtaining nourishment from the radiance of the *Shekhinah* in the same way as eating and drinking would nourish a human being, and he suggests that this is the way Moses was sustained on Sinai.

There will be two levels of existence in the World to Come. One will be for less evolved souls, who require sustenance of some kind, much as manna and miracles sustained the people in the wilderness. The second is for more evolved souls, who will exist like angels, with wings, and roam over the face of the waters.[24]

Nahmanides brings *Gate of Reward* to a close with an extended and respectful discussion of his differences with Maimonides. First, he concludes that the matter of whether there will be bodies in the World to Come is an open question; second, he states his opinion that Maimonides intended to strengthen people's belief in the soul, which is why he placed so much emphasis on it. But Nahmanides respectfully disagrees with Maimonides about the second dying of the resurrected, whose spirit alone enters the World to Come. Instead he submits that his own view is the correct one and appropriately supported by law and tradition: "that the people of the resurrection will exist forever, from the time of the resurrection of the dead to the World to Come, which is an everlasting world."[25]

✡   OTHER MEDIEVAL JEWISH PHILOSOPHERS

The most influential Jewish philosophers who followed Nahmanides were Rabbi Levi ben Gerson (1288–1344, known as Gersonides and by the acronym Ralbag), who lived in southern France, and Hasdai Crescas (ca. 1340–1410), who was born in Barcelona and active as a teacher (though not a rabbi) in Aragon and Saragossa. Neither of the two, in their major works, dealt much with questions of the hereafter: Gersonides was a highly developed rationalist whose idea of immortality seems to have been more bound up with the intellect than with the soul, and Crescas, while he referred to the immortality of the soul and resurrection as binding concepts in Judaism, did not analyze them in depth in his works.

A student of Crescas, philosopher and theologian Joseph Albo (c. 1380–1444), did devote much of his work to questions of the afterlife. Like Nahmanides, Albo lived in Spain and participated in a Jewish/ Christian disputation defending the Jewish faith at Tortosa in 1413–1414. Albo's major work, *The Book of Principles* (*Sefer ha-Ikkarim*), was one of the most popular Jewish books of his generation; he wrote it to explain Jewish views to the Christian world and to support his fellow Jews as they grappled with the persecution that accompanied the Christian reconquest (*reconquista*) of Spain.

Albo was familiar with rabbinic literature and Jewish and Islamic philosophy, as well as mathematics and medicine. In *The Book of Principles*, he gives a rationalistic presentation of Judaism, supporting his arguments with both philosophical and rabbinic citations. His purpose, like that of his predecessors, was to reconcile revelation and reason. Toward this end, Albo attempted to summarize the essence of Judaism in a series of tenets or essential beliefs.

While the reduction of Judaism to a series of principles was not new – Maimonides' Thirteen Principles of Faith serve as the classic example – Albo manages to condense Judaism to the very minimum number of basics. His three principles are:

- The existence of God
- The revelation of the Torah
- Reward and punishment

Under these three headings, Albo sets out the entire framework of Judaism. He identifies six "dogmas" that are also part of the faith, one of which is the resurrection of the dead and another the coming of the Messiah. He also sets out a number of theories about the soul:

> It seems to us that the proper and correct opinion of the Torah is that the soul is a spiritual substance, having the capacity to understand the service of God, and not mere understanding. Hence when a person attains any degree of understanding of God's service, by reason of attaining some idea or notion of God, be it great or small, he immediately attains a certain degree of life in the World to Come.[26]

This idea about the reward for righteous action being some share in the World to Come, however minimal, underpins Albo's subsequent analysis of the subject and is an important element in the conclusions that he reaches.

Albo surveys the conflicting views of Maimonides and Nahmanides and, in concise and useful summaries, represents the two schools of thought regarding resurrection and the World to Come. According to Albo:

> Maimonides [says] … that the persons resurrected will use all their sense functions in the natural way, and then will die again and return to dust.[27] … Then the souls will, by reason of their attainments during the second life, be privileged to enjoy the future world in a higher degree than the one they enjoyed before resurrection.[28]

Albo reiterates Maimonides' "double death" theory and his basic claim that the main reward for the righteous is spiritual, bestowed upon the soul alone in the World to Come.[29]

Concerning Nahmanides' views on resurrection, Albo writes:

> After resurrection, the persons will live as long as their natural capacity permits them, and then their bodies will be transmuted by purification and will become like the body of Elijah. And thenceforth they will continue to exist as body and soul, but will no longer use any sense function, will not eat or drink or die and will remain forever without eating and drinking.[30]

Albo explains Nahmanides' position that in the next world there should be both bodily and spiritual reward after resurrection, even if the body has evolved to a highly spiritualized state.

In his own analysis of the hereafter, Albo interprets the differing views of the two giants of medieval Jewish thought but does not try to reconcile them or even state a preference between them. His most helpful insight is a point he makes about terminology. The rabbis of the Talmud, and also the two philosophers, use the phrase "World to Come" in different senses. In some contexts, it connotes the survival of the soul immediately after death, while in others it connotes life after the resurrection. Maimonides' view of the bodiless, spiritual existence of the soul seems to focus more on the former (the "World to Come" after death – or what Nahmanides calls the "world of souls") and Nahmanides' on the latter (the "World to Come" after resurrection). Albo writes:

> The expression "World to Come" is used both in a broad and a narrow sense. In a broad sense it applies to any degree of reward which the soul gets after death. In a narrow and specific sense it denotes the highest degree that the soul of the perfectly righteous man can attain, a degree which comes after resurrection. . . .
>
> "All Israelites have a share in the World to Come" means that in the world of souls which is after death, every Israelite will attain to some degree according to his conduct. But the highest and last degree – "life in the World to Come" – no one can attain except the perfectly righteous, and that only after the resurrection.[31]

Perhaps Albo is trying to find a position midway between the views of the two sages. On the one hand, when he cites the statement from *Sanhedrin* 10 that "All Israelites have a share in the World to Come," he seems to agree with Maimonides that the World to Come is where souls go after death to receive their reward. On the other hand, he seems attracted to Nahmanides' view that there is a higher level of *olam ha-ba* for only the very pious who are among those who are resurrected. From this presentation, we see that Albo was an eclectic if not original thinker and a skillful popularizer.

Albo was the last great figure in the pantheon of Jewish medieval philosophers who grappled with the demands of reason and revelation in an age when Judaism was alternately esteemed and on the defensive. Contemporaneously with these thinkers, however, another tradition was developing: the tradition of the mystics, which interpreted the rabbinical sources in radically different ways.

Mysticism: Reincarnation in Kabbalah

A T THE SAME time as the theologians described in the previous chapter were developing their ideas about the afterlife, a mystical tradition, less tied to rationalism and more accepting of the enigmatic and unexplainable, was coming into flower, bringing new, even radical, insights to the Jewish view of the soul. The leading proponents of the mystical tradition saw human transformation as a process brought about not only by adherence to Jewish law but by supersensory events that they felt allowed them to have a direct and personal experience of the Divine. Their ideas about the afterlife tended to be more personal as well.

Because the mystics experienced God differently from Jews whose connection to the Divine was found almost exclusively in text and prayer, they dealt differently with the concepts of reward, punishment, and the fate of the soul than did their more rationalist contemporaries. This is not to say that mystical Jewish thinkers were unconcerned with Jewish law. Nahmanides, a scholar of Jewish law and commentator on the Torah, also led the Gerona school of mystics in thirteenth-century Spain. Joseph Caro, a practicing mystic who settled in Safed in the sixteenth century, was the author of the *Shulhan Arukh* ("The Set Table"), which still stands today as an authoritative code of Jewish law and religious practice for Orthodox Jews. While some of the mystical thinkers of Judaism were distant from the normative Judaism of their day, others were very much part of the mainstream, well versed in Torah and teachings that had preceded them. This gave their insights deep roots in sacred texts as well as mystical experiences.

The Jewish mystical tradition, known generally by the name Kabbalah,[1] evolved gradually over more than a millennium. Scholars trace it back to the first century C.E., where a body of speculation known as the *Ma'aseh Merkavah* ("The Work of the Chariot") emerged. Based on an exegesis of Ezekiel's chariot vision at the beginning of the biblical book that bears his name, *Ma'aseh Merkavah* describes the soul's ascent through the heavenly spheres to behold a vision of the chariot, which bears God's throne of glory. Such speculation on esoteric matters continued through the tannaitic and talmudic eras. A well-known parable in the Talmud (*Hagigah* 14a) describes the fate of four rabbis of the first century who entered a garden to search out the mysteries of God's ways. The term used for the garden, *pardes,* refers to the phenomenon of mystical experience. The parable tells us that of the four rabbis, one died, one went insane, one became a heretic, and only one, Rabbi Akiva, "went in whole and came out whole" – suggesting that mystical encounters were indeed dangerous and powerful experiences.

The next main work of Jewish mysticism was the *Sefer Yetzirah* ("The Book of Creation"), an anonymous work composed between the third and sixth centuries that described the creation of the universe through the letters of the Hebrew alphabet. *Sefer ha-Bahir* ("The Book of Brightness"), which appeared in Provence, France, at the end of the twelfth century (though many attribute it to a *tanna* of the first century), represents a significant development in the Jewish mystical tradition in that it is the first work to allude to the major symbols of the Kabbalah. It also contains the first reference to the transmigration of souls.

By the thirteenth century, Jewish mysticism truly began to flower, and its tradition was sufficiently established for a mystical commentary on the Pentateuch to be produced. Known as the *Zohar* ("The Book of Splendor"), this work was ascribed to the second-century talmudic sage, Shimon bar Yohai,[2] and his contemporaries, though Gershom Scholem, the leading modern scholar of Jewish mysticism, posits that its author was most likely the thirteenth-century Spanish kabbalist Moses de Leon.

Written in scholarly Aramaic, the *Zohar* sets out the concepts that even today are recognized as central to Jewish mysticism, such as the idea that everything in the universe is related by spiritual energy to everything else. It introduces its own symbolism, such as the "Tree of Life," an expression that generally refers to the written Torah but here signifies the life force infusing all existence and the mystical aspects of Torah as well.[3] The *Zohar* was the first work to describe the ten *sefirot*, the ten "emanations" of divinity (also called "stages" or "crowns") of God's inner world. It also introduced the notion of the hidden and unknowable God, which it calls the *Ein Sof,* meaning "without end" or "infinite." A number of mystical works by various authors came after the *Zohar*, refining its ideas and developing new ones.

The mystical teachers and masters delved deeply into the Torah, the commentaries of the *tannaim* and *amoraim*, and later rabbis' teachings, infusing them with a new vision of the cosmos and God's powers within it. They sought to enhance their understanding of God, reading the texts of the tradition symbolically and interpreting them so as to extract hidden meanings. As the Zohar explains:

> Thus had the Torah not clothed herself in the garments of this world, the world could not endure it. The stories of the Torah are thus only her outer garments, and whoever looks upon that garment as being the Torah itself, woe to that man – such a one will have no portion in the World to Come. (*Zohar*, vol. 5, 152a)[4]

This approach, based on the idea that there is a deeper meaning underneath the surface of reality, led to the evolution of a different vocabulary and a new set of ideas about what happens to the soul in the hereafter.

ℵ THE SOUL'S JOURNEY AFTER DEATH

In the mystic's view, the human soul was part of the spiritual realm before birth and has its own eschatology after death. As a spiritual entity, the human soul is a link between heaven and earth. Likewise, human actions can elevate the soul from its earthly residence to its heavenly origins.

As we have seen in the previous chapter, the rationalist Jewish philosophers had a highly developed concept of the immortality of the soul. Both Sa'adiah and Maimonides subscribed to the idea of a soul with multiple aspects. But from the *Zohar* onward, we find mystical thinkers reconsidering earlier sages' definitions of the soul and making them not only more complex but also more dynamic and personal. In particular, we find teachings that describe each aspect of the soul undergoing a separate destiny in the afterlife.

There are three words for "soul" in Hebrew that provide the springboard for the new mystical conception of immortality. The *Zohar* describes them as follows:

> Now the soul is a compound of three grades, and hence it has three names, to wit, *nefesh* (vital principle) *ruach* (spirit) and *neshamah* (soul proper). *Nefesh* is the lowest of the three, *ruach* is a grade higher, whilst *neshamah* is the highest of all and dominates the others.
> (*Zohar*, vol. 2, 205b–206a)[5]

All three aspects – *nefesh, ruah* and *neshamah* – are understood to be part of the soul's essential unity. In another passage from the *Zohar*, the terms are defined with reference to this biblical verse: "With my soul have I desired you in the night; yea, with my spirit within me will I seek you early" (Isaiah 26:9). The *nefesh* is understood to rule by night and the *ruah* by day, while the *neshamah* rules over both. All three aspects work in cooperation during one's lifetime, but the mystical tradition posits that each of the separate aspects of the soul undergoes a different destiny after death.

Nefesh

The *nefesh* is roughly equivalent to the "life force," the vital part of a person that is instilled into every human being at birth. After death, the *nefesh* stays with the body in the grave. Then, in a process that lasts from three to seven days, the soul extricates itself from the body. The more attached the *nefesh* was to the physical world, the more difficult and painful this separation, so the sensualist has a harder time of it than the more spiritually inclined person. The *nefesh* shuttles between the grave and its previous home, mourning the death of the body and saddened by the grief of those it left behind. It "roams to and fro through the world" while the body resolves itself into dust and suffers terrible torment when it sees the body that once housed it decomposing. The *Zohar* describes the aftermath of death as an arduous process:

> Indeed, what a number of ordeals man has to undergo in passing out of the world! First comes the ordeal from on high, at the moment when the spirit leaves the body . . . then comes his ordeal when his actions and utterances precede him and make proclamation concerning him. Another ordeal is when he enters the tomb. One more is in the tomb itself. He afterwards undergoes an ordeal at the hands of the worms. There is then the ordeal of
> *Gehinnom.*   (*Zohar*, vol. 5, 126b–127a)[6]

The *nefesh,* the mystics postulate, is the part of the soul that migrates into other bodies in reincarnation.

Ruah

The *ruah,* generally translated as "spirit," is the aspect of the soul that governs the intellect and moral values. It has a basic ability to distinguish between good and evil and can persuade a person to act in either direction. Perhaps because it bears this responsibility, the *ruah* is consigned to *Gehinnom* after death. Other teachings, which we will encounter later, suggest that the *ruhot* (spirits) of individuals who lived ethically and spiritually upright lives are spared the ordeal of *Gehinnom* entirely.

The *Zohar* has rich descriptions of *Gehinnom*. The seven-tiered system we saw in Nahmanides' writings appears here also, with vivid descriptions of the journey the soul undergoes. An angel receives the *ruah* and delivers it into the appropriate tier of *Gehinnom*, where it is purified by fire for twelve months. The angel's name, Dumah, means "silence" in Hebrew, yet this angel apparently has much authority over the residents of *Gehinnom*.

> There are in *Gehinnom* seven circuits and seven gates, each with several gatekeepers under their own chiefs. The souls of sinners are delivered by Dumah to those gate-keepers, who then close the gates of flaming fire . . . .
> (*Zohar*, vol. 2, 237b)[7]

There is respite on the Sabbath, the passage continues, when there is no fire, because of the prohibition against kindling fire on the Sabbath. However, when the Sabbath ends, the punishment continues: "a herald proclaims at each gate, 'Let the wicked go back to Sheol.'"[8]

The *Zohar* also deals with the fate of the souls of those who were so sinful that they cannot ascend. These souls are sent to an area known as "the boiling filth," which they never leave:

> There are certain sinners who pollute themselves over and over again by their own sins and are never purified. They die without repentance . . . . These are they who are condemned forever to remain in the place of "boiling filth" and never leave it . . . .
>
> On Sabbaths, New Moons and festivals the fire is extinguished there, and they have a respite from punishment, but unlike sinners of a lesser degree who are accorded relief, they are not allowed to leave that place even on such days.　　　　(*Zohar*, vol. 4, 150b)[9]

The stint in *Gehinnom* is finite unless one was terribly wicked while on earth. The purification that occurs in the underworld prepares the *ruah* for the next stage of its journey. It ascends to a place known as "*Gan Eden shel mata,*" or the Lower Garden of Eden, where it is greeted by none other than Adam himself. The *ruah* then is cleansed in a river of light and acquires what is described as a "vestment" – a celestial covering that replaces its original body. The vestment is understood as being the very same one the soul initially had to take off in order to be born into a physical body upon earth:

> This place is the abode of the holy spirits, both of those that have come into this world and also of those that have not yet come into this world. ... When the time comes for the spirit to leave this world again, it cannot do so until the Angel of Death has taken off the garment of the body. When that has been done, he again puts on that other garment in the Garden of Eden of which he had to divest himself when he entered this world. ... In it he rests and moves, and contemplates continually the supernal mysteries which, when he was in the earthly body, he could neither grasp nor understand.
>
> (*Zohar*, vol. 4, 150a)[10]

Clothed once again in its celestial vestment, the *ruah* is able to enjoy the delights of the Garden, including visions of the divine emanation.[11] Eventually the *ruah* will leave the Lower Garden, pass once again through a river of light and ascend to the Higher Garden, the home of the *neshamah*.

Neshamah

This is the highest level of the soul, the divine spark. *Neshamah* is the part of the soul that occupies itself with Torah, that strives to reunite itself with its divine source, and that is wholly good.

The mystical tradition believes that the *neshamah* exists prior to birth.

There is a teaching that all souls are woven into a curtain that hangs before God's throne of glory. This curtain records both the history and the destiny of every soul. Thus, for the mystics, the journey of the *neshamah* after death is only one aspect of a larger cycle actually begun prior to birth.

When a person dies, the *neshamah*, being wholly good, does not need to be punished. It ascends directly to the Higher Garden of Eden, which is believed to be the place it came from originally. It never comes down to earth again. The Higher Garden of Eden is as different from the lower one, according to the *Zohar*, as darkness is to light.

> [The souls] stay [in lower *Gan Eden*] for a time, then rise in the air and ascend to the celestial Academy, which is the higher *Gan Eden*; then they rise again and bathe in the dewy rivers of pure balsam and then descend and remain below, and sometimes they appear to men to perform for them miracles in the manner of angels . . . .
> (*Zohar*, vol. 1, 7a)[12]

The *neshamah* is also clothed in a garment, but, in contrast to that of the *ruah*, this garment is of the very finest quality, since it is woven from the zeal and devotion the individual brought to prayer and Torah study. We can observe, in passing, how once again the afterlife is being used to encourage appropriate behavior while on earth. In a similar vein, we find that the Higher Garden is organized into study circles in which the soul delights itself with learning about the nature of God. The study circles are of various levels, reflecting the spiritual attainments of those who inhabit them.

There is one final destination for the soul called *tzeror ha-hayyim*, or "the bundle of life," a name taken from I Samuel 25:29. The phrase *tzeror ha-hayyim* has resonance for most Jews from its appearance in the mourners' prayer, *El Malei Rahamim*, expressing the hope that the soul will continue to live under God's protection. Mystics envisioned *tzeror ha-hayyim* as a place superior to the Higher Garden as well as a kind of divine clearinghouse for souls where they are assigned their next incarnations.

⚘   REINCARNATION

Reincarnation is known in Hebrew as *gilgul*, which means "circularity." For the Jewish mystical tradition the term has a special meaning: that of metempsychosis, the transmigration of the soul after death to another body for rebirth. The idea of reincarnation, which is found in religious traditions around the world, is not original to the Jews. The Jewish mystical tradition, however, reconfigured and remolded it to fit with Judaism. Reincarnation was a very late arrival on the scene of Jewish ideas. Neither the Bible, the Talmud, nor the Midrash says anything at all on the subject. Sa'adiah rejected the doctrine as "madness and confusion"; Maimonides did not mention it at all.[13] Nevertheless, reincarnation is frequently discussed in Jewish literature of the Middle Ages. As noted earlier, the concept is first mentioned in the *Sefer ha-Bahir*, although the term *gilgul* is not yet used to describe the phenomenon.

Sefer ha-Bahir suggests that the soul is not lent to a human being for one incarnation only. Instead, it continues to migrate from body to body:

> When Israel is good, then [the east] is the place from which I will bring your seed, and new seed will be granted to you. But if Israel is wicked, [then I will bring] seed that has already been in the world. It is thus written, "A generation goes and a generation comes" [Ecclesiastes 1:4], teaching us that it has already come.
>
> (*Sefer ha-Bahir*, Part 1, 155).[14]

A distinction is drawn in *Sefer ha-Bahir* between "new" souls and "old" souls. The Messiah is a new soul but cannot become incarnate until all of the old souls, which are rolling around in the world, passing from body to body, have become clean. Only then can new souls descend from their place on high:

> When Israel is good, these [new] souls are worthy of emerging and coming to this world. But if they are not

good, then [these souls] do not emerge. We therefore say, "The Son of David will not come until all the souls in the body are completed."

What is the meaning of "all the souls in the body"? We say this refers to all the souls in man's body. [When these are completed], new ones will be worthy of emerging. The Son of David (the Messiah) will then come. He will be able to be born, since his soul will emerge among the other new souls.   (*Sefer ha-Bahir* Part 1, 184)[15]

There is also a brief discussion of reward and punishment that implies that souls live more than once:

Why is there a righteous person who has good and [another] righteous person who has evil? This is because the second righteous person was wicked previously and is now being punished.   (*Sefer ha-Bahir*, Part 1, 195)[16]

In the thirteenth century the doctrine of reincarnation developed further. Some Spanish kabbalists, such as Nahmanides, seem to be cautious about mentioning it and only do so by hints and allusions. The situation is entirely different in the *Zohar*, where the subject is dealt with openly and at considerable length. It is here, too, that the word *gilgul*, to indicate the transmigration of souls, is used for the first time.

As it unfolds, the *Zohar* expands the notion of *gilgul* to encompass all of human experience. Initially it assigns transmigration as a fate for limited categories of sin: notably, those who committed sexual transgressions or who failed to procreate:

Now the spirit which has left this world without procreation and engendering of children undergoes constant transmigration, finding no rest and rolling about "like a stone inside a sling" until a redeemer comes forward to redeem it and bring it back to the same vessel which it formerly used, and to which it clave with heart and

soul, as to its life's partner, in the union of spirit with
spirit.   (*Zohar*, vol. 3, 99b)[17]

But the *Zohar* also discusses reincarnation as something that happens
to all human souls:

> Truly, all souls must undergo transmigration; but men do
> not perceive the ways of the Holy One, how the revolving
> scale is set up and men are judged every day at all times,
> and how they are brought before the tribunal, both before
> they enter into this world and after they leave it.
>   (*Zohar*, vol. 3, 99b)[18]

In another passage, the transmigration of souls is compared to the
beneficial forces of nature as an example of God's mission to perfect the
world:

> So God has planted trees in this world: if they prosper,
> well and good, and if not, He uproots them and replants
> them time after time. All the ways of the Holy One are
> thus for the purpose of achieving good and the perfec-
> tion of the world.   (*Zohar*, vol. 2, 187b)[19]

The *Zohar* also focuses on the importance of appropriate behavior in
this life, which will dictate what will happen after death:

> It is the path taken by man in this world that determines
> the path of the soul on [its] departure. Thus, if a man is
> drawn towards the Holy One and is filled with longing
> towards Him in this world, the soul in departing from
> him is carried upward towards the higher realms by the
> impetus given [it] each day in this world. . . . If a man fol-
> lows a certain direction in this world, he will be led rather
> in the same direction when he departs: . . . if holy, holy,
> and if defiled, defiled.   (*Zohar*, vol. 1, 99b–100a)[20]

In other words, reincarnation is not just a punishment but also a process whose goal is purification. A person who does not behave appropriately while alive should expect to be made to live again after death, with the opportunity to make a better job of it the second (or third) time around.

No sooner had the *Zohar* begun circulating than kabbalists began to expand the doctrine of reincarnation, widening the categories of persons whose souls were subject to transmigration. Kabbalists writing in response to the *Zohar* included not only the wicked but also the *benonim* ("in-betweeners"), those who were neither wicked nor good, as candidates for reincarnation. By the fourteenth century, scholars were also suggesting that the righteous would be reincarnated endlessly, this time for the benefit of the world.

This expansion might have been due to the compelling and flexible nature of the doctrine of transmigration. It could be used to demand appropriate behavior in this life, or to reward the righteous with opportunities to guide others. In either case, it provides consolation to those who fear that death is final. With reincarnation, one will get the opportunity to live once more. That life will not be led in some remote coming age, but in the world as we know it, and it may well happen quite soon.

The number of reincarnations for the purpose of purging sin is generally limited to three, based on a kabbalistic reading of Job 33:29–30:

> Truly God does all these things
> Two or three times to a man,
> To return his soul from the Pit
> That he may be lit up with the light of the living.

The kabbalists believed that if the soul persisted in returning to its evil ways after three reincarnations, it would be condemned to *Gehinnom*. Others, however, thought that a soul could not migrate to a new incarnation until it had been punished and purified in *Gehinnom*. Those who believed that righteous souls also were reincarnated assigned those souls to *Gan Eden* for reward before they found new homes. Eventually, during this post-Zoharic period, a belief in near-universal reincarnation became the normative view among kabbalists. Only the supremely right-eous, they thought, were exempt from having their souls sent back to earth, though *tzaddikim* could choose to return for the sake of improving the world.[21]

The *Zohar* also addresses the question of resurrection, which posed a problem in logic for the kabbalists. On the one hand, as Maimonides insisted, belief in resurrection is central to Judaism. On the other hand, if the soul has transmigrated, into which body would it be resurrected? The question is not resolved, but the *Zohar* records three possibilities:

- Rabbi Hizkiah believes that the soul returns to the last body it inhabited, with the bodies in which it had lived previously regarded as though they had not been.
- Rabbi Isaac believes that God will provide other spirits for the bodies that are left without souls.
- Rabbi Eleazar believes that upon resurrection every soul will bear a form identical to the one it wore in the world (which suggests that somehow extra bodies will be provided).[22]

As the *Zohar*'s ideas began to circulate widely over the next two centuries, scholars continued to develop the idea of the reincarnation and multiple aspects of the soul. In this period the soul came to be understood as being composed of fragments, giving off "soul sparks" (*nitzotzot*) in the way that a candle gives off many sparks. This, incidentally, solves the dilemma of resurrection; according to this school of thought, each body into which the soul migrates could be reinfused with a single spark from the multiple soul.

Souls might also cluster into family units through soul sparks. This idea was used to justify levirate marriage, the biblically prescribed practice requiring a man to marry his brother's widow if she had not borne him sons to carry on his name. The mystics now suggested that the son born to the man who married his dead brother's wife was in fact a reincarnation of the first husband's soul.

𝄢   THE KABBALAH OF ISAAC LURIA

The expulsion of the Jewish community from Spain in 1492, and from Portugal shortly thereafter, forced Sephardic Jews to flee the Iberian Peninsula and relocate. Among them, proponents of Kabbalah were dispersed throughout Europe and the Middle East. By the sixteenth century, several mystical scholars formed a new center in the town of Safed in northern Palestine, with Rabbi Isaac Luria as their inspired and charismatic leader.

Luria, known as the Ari (the Lion) and the Arizal (*zal* meaning of blessed memory), was born in Jerusalem in 1534 and lived a tragically short life, dying in Safed in 1572 at the age of thirty-eight after a plague broke out. He was initially trained as a rabbi, but in his early twenties he became involved in studying the *Zohar,* and from then on he became a recluse who, as he later recounted, was frequently visited by prophets, particularly the prophet Elijah. He considered his own soul to be related to that of Rabbi Shimon bar Yohai (traditionally regarded as the author of the *Zohar*) and believed himself one of the last reincarnations of Moses.

Luria's teachings were recorded by his disciple, Hayyim Vital. Within his circle of students at Safed were figures who later became famous teachers and scholars in their own right, such as Joseph Caro, author of the *Shulhan Arukh*, and Rabbi Moses Cordovero.

Luria's influence upon Judaism remains noticeable even today. He and his circle in Safed, believing that every single commandment had a mystical dimension, created the tradition of going out to the fields to welcome the Sabbath like a bride, an idea reflected in the Friday night service, *Kabbalat Shabbat* ("Receiving the Sabbath"). His pupil, Rabbi Shlomo Alkabetz, wrote the famous hymn *Lekha Dodi* ("Come, My Beloved"), which still forms part of the *Kabbalat Shabbat* liturgy. Moreover, the tradition of remaining awake all night to study on the first night of Shavuot (the festival that celebrates God's gift of Torah to the Israelites) came from Luria, as did the practice of welcoming *ushpizin*, invisible guests from the Jewish past, into one's *sukkah* at Sukkot (the fall festival of booths).

One major difference between Luria and the mystical tradition that preceded him was his focus on the problem of evil in the world. Modern scholars would later suggest that the pain of exile suffered by most Jews was integral to Luria's understanding of the fragmentary nature of the world and informed every aspect of his approach to Judaism and spirituality.

Although Luria spent his brief life in Palestine, the knowledge that most Jews lived in *galut* – exile from Zion – was a guiding beacon of his philosophy. (Only a few thousand Jews lived in Ottoman-ruled Palestine in the mid-sixteenth century.) To Luria, *galut* was a metaphor for the entire world and that the Jews, who lived in physical exile, stood as a symbol of the human exile from a righteous world. Even the *Shekhinah*, the feminine emanation of God, was in exile with the Jews, her separation from God mirrored in the Jews' exile from Zion.

Luria's brand of Kabbalah brought much comfort to a people that had experienced exile again and again in its history, encouraging Jews to imagine that even their Creator could identify with the concept of exile. The Lurianic Kabbalah brought a measure of liberation and spiritual salvation to people who had suffered greatly. As we shall see, it also gave them an active role in repairing the world's brokenness and restoring wholeness to the cosmic order.

Creation and the Breaking of the Vessels

Luria's ideas about the afterlife are part of a much broader understanding of the origins of the universe and the goal of human life. At the heart of his doctrine is an original and revolutionary theory of creation. Luria taught that creation was not an emanatory process from the *Ein Sof*, the infinite source of power and light, as the kabbalists before him believed, but rather began in an act of divine contraction (*tzimtzum*): God contracted Himself in order to create space for a created world. After the *tzimtzum*, a ray of light flowed out of the Godhead and took the shape of *Adam Kadmon*, a spiritual version of primordial man. According to Luria, God sent out His divine light through *Adam Kadmon*'s eyes, ears, nose, and mouth; these emanations became the ten *sefirot*, the ten cosmic aspects of divinity described in Kabbalah.

But the divine light that emerged from *Adam Kadmon* was too strong for the vessels meant to hold it and the vessels shattered, scattering the holy sparks throughout the universe. Some returned to their divine source, but others were trapped in the earthly shards.[23] This cosmic calamity, called "the breaking of the vessels" (*shevirat hakeilim*), occurred because the *Ein Sof's* infiniteness could not be contained, but there is also a human parallel to this cosmic event.

The divine sparks were initially supposed to work together to repair the world, but Adam, in his human form, thwarted that goal, at least temporarily, when he disobeyed God by eating from the Tree of Knowledge. Thus the cosmic mishap had an earthly parallel in this breach in relationship. The Lurianic Kabbalah teaches that when Adam sinned, the cosmic unity was broken. At the same time, Luria taught that Jews could play a definite role in the redemption of the world through their religious life. Observing the commandments would help to elevate the sparks and allow them to return to their source and eventually reconstitute the body of *Adam Kadmon*.

This theory of *tikkun*, the repair of the universe, is fundamental to Luria's teachings both on cosmological and human levels. Redemption was to be effected by gathering the scattered holy sparks and restoring them to their proper place. This image is also a powerful reflection of the longing of diaspora Jews for ingathering in Zion and the end of exile.

Perfecting the Human Soul

The concept of *tikkun* is tied to that of *gilgul*, the transmigration of souls, in that *tikkun* involves not only gathering dispersed divine sparks but also returning human souls to their proper places. For Luria, the transmigration of souls is an important component in the healing of the divine order.

According to Luria, there are four mystical "worlds" or "dimensions" between God and the earthly cosmos. The highest is the world of *Atzilut* ("emanation"); beneath it is the world of *Beri'ah* ("creation"); the third is *Yetzirah* ("formation") and the fourth is *Asiyah* ("action/concretization"). Above all four worlds is the realm of God and *Adam Kadmon*, primordial man created in God's image. As the divine energy travels down through the four worlds to the earthly *Asiyah*, its holiness is progressively reduced. At the same time, there is the potential for humans to engage in a restorative process and climb back up this ladder of ascent toward holiness. In a sense, these mystical worlds straddle the realms of life and death in that human beings struggle to perfect themselves in this life in preparation for the next.

Different parts of the soul are associated with each of these four worlds. In addition to *nefesh, ruah,* and *neshamah,* Luria posits two other aspects of the soul, *hayah* ("life" or "living essence") and *yehidah* ("unity" or "unique essence"), which correspond to the world of *Atzilut.* The highest level of the soul, *yehidah* also corresponds to *Adam Kadmon,* the most majestic vessel of divine glory.[24]

> *Atzilut* (Emanation) — *Yehidah* (Unity) / *Hayah* (Life)
> *Beri'ah* (Creation) — *Neshamah* (Breath)
> *Yetzirah* (Formation) — *Ruah* (Spirit)
> *Asiyah* (Action) — *Nefesh* (Will)

The purpose of life is for human beings gradually to perfect every level of their souls in order to ascend through all the four worlds:

> It is necessary that each person correct all the aspects of the world of *Asiyah* before ascending to receive the higher level of soul and world . . . . What does this mean in practicality? The man must occupy himself in the law and its commandments applicable to the entire world of *Asiyah* and not only what is connected to the source of his soul. This includes even accomplishing the commandments that he finds difficult.[25]

Luria taught that the human soul is able to ascend through these practices: the commandments (*mitzvot*), actions, and prayer. The principal time of day in which to elevate one's soul, according to Luria, is during the *Tahanun* prayer, the supplications recited after the *Amidah,* the central prayer of the traditional morning service. The *Tahanun,* a series of requests for grace and assistance that goes back to Temple times, is also called *nefilat apayim*, "falling on the face," because through the talmudic period at least, the practice was for worshipers to prostrate themselves fully when reciting the first part of *Tahanun*.[26] This posture continued to be used in some Jewish communities into medieval times, and scholars suggest that Luria and other mystics of his day embraced prostration during *Tahanun* not only to humble themselves before God, but to mimic the posture of death, which would enable their souls to become purified.

> In other words, the kabbalist, at his most vulnerable moment, the confession of sin, stands fully exposed and ready to accept the consequences of his deeds – death itself. . . . Only divine mercy enables him to survive intact, his sins having been expiated through a momentary experience of voluntary death. Unsatisfied with the partial atonement possible in this world, a person chooses mystical death as a means of achieving total purification of the soul, otherwise available only through physical death.[27]

The implication, then, might be that this experience of mystical death leads to a mystical form of reincarnation.

In other areas of life also, Luria said, one should strive to attain purity, since only if one is pure can one achieve a higher level of holiness. Devotion in prayer, attention to ritual detail (such as the recitation of blessings with the proper intention), and concentration on fulfilling the commandments are all required. Nonetheless, the work of elevation may not be completed by the time a person dies. If not, he will be reincarnated in order for the process to continue: "If [a] man will not correct his soul of *Nefesh* completely the first time and will die with an incomplete *Nefesh*, this *Nefesh* will have to return in reincarnation various times until it is completely cleansed."[28]

Luria's Kabbalah reinterprets an ancient midrash to suggest that every human soul is a spark from the soul of *Adam Kadmon*. *Adam Kadmon* was conceived as having no bodily form but instead as a cosmic individual, each of whose five soul dimensions – *nefesh, ruah, neshamah, hayah*, and *yehidah* – was subdivided into 613 "roots" corresponding to the 613 commandments. Each root then sprouted smaller roots, so each of the levels of *Adam Kadmon's* soul comprised thousands of "soul sparks."[29] If people behave well, they will be able to reintegrate the soul sparks. But if they do not, they will be destined to reincarnate again and again until the sparks are reunited.

Here Luria departs from the *Zohar's* claim that reincarnation is limited to three cycles. As far as Luria is concerned, the soul's destiny is to be reincarnated again and again until it has risen through every single one of the five worlds. Any sin returns a person to the starting point at the base of the system from which he must begin all over again unless he repents. If he does, God accepts his repentance and, depending on the severity of the sin, forgives the sinner or allows him to begin the process of atonement.[30]

It seems clear that this type of reincarnation, as in the *Zohar,* is still serving some kind of punitive function. Indeed, in contrast to earlier teachings about reincarnation, it is perfectly possible for people to be reincarnated as animals, plants, or even rocks, in order to cleanse them of the sins they committed as humans, as seen in this anecdote:

> Rabbi Chaim Vital was with the Arizal [Luria] many times when they walked in the fields, and the Arizal related to him that "this man by this name who was a righteous scholar, because of a particular sin, is reincarnated now in this rock, or this plant, and so on."[31]

Luria also described another form of reincarnation that would help a disembodied soul attain what he did not achieve in life. This involves a special category of reincarnation known as *ibbur* ("pregnancy"), in which a body with an existing soul is "impregnated" temporarily with another soul (in contrast to *gilgul,* in which the soul of someone who has died migrates to someone just being born and remains with that person for his entire life).

In some cases, the visiting soul is seeking to perfect itself: to atone for a sin it committed in the past or to fulfill a *mitzvah* it had failed to fulfill in its previous incarnation. Sometimes, though, *ibbur* occurs in order to elevate the living individual, to help that person complete a particular task or fulfill a commandment. It should be noted that in *ibbur,* even when the visiting soul had an issue of sin or *mitzvah* it needed to resolve, it was usually the soul of someone striving to become, or was close to becoming, a fully righteous person – not that of someone who had committed a long list of sins or had failed to observe many of the commandments.

Luria and his followers also believed that the soul of a wicked person could visit a living person and inhabit his body. Anyone possessed by such a *ruah ra'ah* ("wicked spirit") was considered to be a perpetrator of sin himself. Such spirits required exorcism for removal. During the seventeenth century, the wandering or evil spirit who took possession of a person became known in Yiddish folklore as a *dybbuk,* from its practice of clinging to a living person.

The Lurianic kabbalists, like their earlier counterparts, believed that many biblical characters experienced reincarnation and showed up as different characters later. In fact, the *Zohar* describes several pious figures in the Bible who experienced a form of *ibbur* at turning points in their lives.[32] Elsewhere in early Kabbalah, Abel is said to have been murdered because he misinterpreted his relationship with the Divine and was given the opportunity to repair this breach – to find his *tikkun* – by being reincarnated as Moses, whose vision of the Divine in the bush is in its pure form. Similarly, the murderous Cain is reincarnated as the benign, helpful Jethro, Moses' father-in-law, rehabilitating his earlier incarnation so that his soul can join the Jewish mainstream.[33]

Luria and his disciples also believed that they themselves were the reincarnations of biblical personages whose souls had migrated through generation after generation of Jewish leaders and, later, prominent rabbis. Luria believed himself to be the reincarnation of Adam, Abel, Moses, and Rabbi Shimon bar Yohai (Rashbi), the *tanna* credited with writing the Zohar.[34] Hayyim Vital claimed his soul had been resident in a long chain of leaders and scholars that included Samuel, Elijah, King Hezekiah, Matityahu the Hasmonean, Rabbi Yohanan ben Zakkai, Rabbi Akiva, and Rabban Gamaliel, among dozens of others.[35]

The disciples and subsequent followers of Luria maintained that he was able to talk with the souls of the dead. Vital describes him, in *Sefer ha-Hezyonot,* as having attained sufficient holiness to receive visitations from the prophet Elijah, who instructed him in mystical wisdom and, when Luria was thirty-six years old, told him to move to Safed.[36] Luria "then increased his piety, asceticism, purity, and holiness until he reached a level where Elijah would constantly reveal himself to him, speaking to him 'mouth to mouth,'" Vital wrote.[37] Also ascribed to Luria were the ability to see angels and the souls of other departed prophets and sages, and the gift of discerning human souls in objects and even sounds found in nature.[38]

Gilgul and Resurrection

Like the *Zohar,* Luria wrestles with the question of which bodies will house migrating souls and be resurrected, formulating a doctrine of resurrection that is even more complex and contradictory than that of the *Zohar*. In some places, Luria suggests that multiple soul sparks can inhabit a single body. In others, he says that even though some soul sparks might have finished their journey of transmigration, they stick together with others of their "family" who are still on the journey, waiting patiently for all of them to complete their mission.

He also teaches that in each lifetime, an individual perfects a single one of the soul sparks, which will then reinvest in that particular body at the time of the resurrection. The same will happen with each of the other soul sparks. Thus all of the bodies inhabited by a multipartite soul will be resurrected (except for those of heretics, whose bodies decay):

> [A man's] body is not lost after death, and his soul is reincarnated in a second body. A spark from the source of the man in his previous life enters into this second body, where the soul is connected with a portion of the spark of the man in his first body.[39]

There are limited discussions of what the resurrection will be like. Luria seems to envisage that it will take place when evil has been purged from the world. At that point Moses himself will be reincarnated, as will the entire generation of Israelites who left Egypt with him.

With the resurrection of the dead, it will be possible for souls of the highest of the kabbalistic worlds, at present estranged from the earth, to return:

> Today we only have the strength to draw down new souls from the worlds of *Beriah, Yetzirah* and *Assiyah* . . . but not from the higher world of *Atzilut* . . . . In the future, after the resurrection of the dead, will be born new souls of the higher category from the world of *Atzilut,* such as the soul of Adam, the first man.

Luria foresaw a time of redemption in which souls from all four mystical worlds, including the realm of divine emanation, would be resurrected and live on.

From these attempts to resolve the conflicts between resurrection and reincarnation – or at least figure out the mechanics of what will occur – we can see that bodily resurrection remained a fundamental tenet of Jewish belief, though somewhat upstaged by reincarnation in Lurianic teachings.

Far more significant in its impact on future generations, however, was Luria's doctrine of the human role in bringing about the era of messianic redemption.

Lurianic Messianism

We will examine the role of the Messiah, or redeemer, in Jewish belief in Chapter 8, but here we will take a brief look at a sudden outburst of messianism that occurred in the second half of the seventeenth century because it is also part of the story of Jewish mysticism. The concept of the Messiah, rooted in the concept of the biblical "king" who would lead the Jews to redemption, was intrinsic to Jewish hopes and aspirations for the future. Coupled with the hope for redemption was often an understanding that present-day woes and persecution represented the "birth pangs of the Messiah" – in other words, that the community's suffering at present would be supplanted by a greater good to come. For example, Luria's followers held that Luria himself was fulfilling a messianic role and that his teachings had a redemptive function.[40] We can see that this attitude leaves people vulnerable to exploitation by false messiahs, and indeed the sixteenth and seventeenth centuries were marked by this phenomenon.

The greatest manifestation of a false messiah took place in the mid-1600s with the appearance of Shabbetai Tzvi. Born in Smyrna (now Izmir, Turkey), he gained a following in Sephardic communities across Europe and in Ashkenazic communities as well following the brutal Chmielnicki massacres in 1648 in Poland and the Ukraine.[41] In 1665, Nathan of Gaza, his self-appointed prophet,[42] declared him to be the Messiah. His fame spread rapidly throughout the Jewish world, with many going so far as to sell their homes in order to follow him to Palestine at a moment's notice. In his apocalyptic message, Shabbetai Tzvi sometimes engaged in antinomian practices in direct violation of Jewish law, causing great dissension within communities. In 1666, when he went to Constantinople to claim his kingdom from the sultan, he was arrested and imprisoned. To the shock of all of his followers, he converted to Islam in order to save his life. The result of his apostasy was a moral void as his followers struggled to come to terms with the betrayal of their hopes. Despite the false messiah debacle, the generation of Jews after Shabbetai Tzvi continued to embrace the idea of the Messiah, but in a different form, with the next major mystical movement, Hasidism.

𝕏   HASIDISM: MYSTICISM FOR THE MASSES

Hasidism traces its roots to a Polish folk preacher and itinerant healer, Rabbi Israel ben Eliezer (c. 1700–1760), more usually known as the Baal Shem Tov ("Master of the Good Name") or the acronym Besht. The movement he began spread rapidly, and by the end of the nineteenth century, hasidic dynasties had been founded all over Eastern Europe.

It is difficult to ascertain hard facts about the Besht's life. What is known beyond doubt, though, is that he was a powerfully influential teacher with a charismatic personality. He preached at a time when most Jews were too poor to spare the time to study sacred texts and were estranged from Jewish leaders who taught that only deep examination and knowledge of the sacred texts would bring Jews close to God. The Besht, in contrast, told his followers that communion with God did not necessarily flow from scholarship but was available to any Jew, educated or not. He and his successors opened up Jewish mysticism to the masses by declaring that mystical union with God was not just reserved for the scholarly elite or ascetics but was available to every human being. He also taught that the acts of simple, pious Jews contributed to *tikkun,* the repair of the world, which would lead to coming of the Messiah.

Scholars have pointed out that Hasidism absorbed a good many of Luria's teachings, but the Besht adapted and expanded them to suit the needs of a much wider and less elite audience. Luria's theories concerning creation, repair of the world, and reincarnation form a substratum of hasidic theology.[43] Central to hasidic belief remained the idea that this world is an emanation from a higher world and that it is a human task to liberate the holy sparks and elevate them to their source on high. In this way, Hasidism converts Luria's complex and esoteric cosmology into a simple, uplifting vision with a practical component for daily life.

Unlike Luria, who presided over an ascetic community of mystics, Hasidism taught that Jews could connect to God through enthusiastic, ecstatic prayer. Singing, dancing, and shouting were all ways that Jews could achieve *devekut,* attachment or cleaving to God, which is the goal of the mystic's religious practice. Although joy and enthusiasm in Jewish prayer were hardly new teachings – the mandate to "make a joyful noise unto the Lord" goes back to the Psalmist – the Besht and other hasidic leaders reinterpreted these doctrines to a radical degree.

Hasidism's apparent focus on prayer over study sparked a counter-movement when the leading rabbinical scholar of his time, the Gaon of Vilna in Lithuania, declared the *hasidim* (followers of Hasidism) a heretical sect. The opponents of Hasidism, known as *mitnagdim* (literally, "opponents") probably were motivated by discomfort not only with the exuberance of hasidic worship but by the charisma and popularity of the Besht, fearing, albeit groundlessly, that he presented an echo of Shabbetai Tzvi.

Like the kabbalists, the *hasidim* believed in a migratory soul. Accordingly, the Baal Shem Tov reported in a letter to his brother that on Rosh ha-Shanah of 5507 (1746), his soul ascended into the spiritual worlds. He reached the part of heaven where the soul of the Messiah is lodged, awaiting its descent into the world. The Ba'al Shem Tov asked it, "When will you come?" The soul answered: "When your teachings become publicized and spread to the world."[44]

In the hasidic view, Jews can actively prepare themselves, through prayer infused with *kavanah* ("spiritual intention"), to be ready for the Messiah when he arrives. There is a teaching that the Hebrew word for waiting, *mehakeh*, is an anagram of the word for wisdom, *hokhmah*, which is taken as evidence of the necessity to learn and be patient in preparation for the Messiah's arrival. In this way, the task of *tikkun* is refocused on the individual's self-improvement, and the dangerous aspects of Lurianic messianism are averted.

The major innovation of Hasidism was its espousal of the idea of the *tzaddik,* who functions as a link between heaven and earth as well as a community leader. In classic hasidic thought, the *tzaddik* is the conduit through which divine energy is transmitted. The idea of the *tzaddik* also has its origins in Luria's Kabbalah, which taught that a soul which has refined itself completely can come back down to earth to provide assistance and guidance to less fortunate souls. The hasidic communities transferred this idea to their living spiritual leaders, often to the extent that their followers sometimes believed them to have superhuman powers of prophecy and miracle-working. In particular, they were believed capable of helping individuals to formulate their prayers in the most effective way to liberate the sparks of holiness in their souls.

Hasidim commonly believed that the *tzaddik* of their community, because of his particularly strong *devekut* with God, was an effective intermediary between God and the people. The *tzaddik,* responsible for the community's welfare, spent time among the people, but he always remained attached to the other world so that he could raise people to a higher level of spirituality.

A *hasid* was likely to believe that the *tzaddik* could act as an intercessor upon his death, bargaining in heaven for a less serious punishment than might be his actual due. It was common practice, for instance, to leave a note (a *kvittel*) on the grave of one's *tzaddik* to ask him to pray on one's behalf in the upper worlds. *Hasidim* also believed that long-dead *tzaddikim* could come down from the higher Garden of Eden to visit on joyous occasions.

All of these ideas were woven into folk tales, enabling ordinary people to grasp what previously had been esoteric mystical ideas. One such story, "The Rabbi's Son" by Rabbi Nahman of Bratslav, tells of the son of a rabbi who feels something is missing in his prayer and wants to consult a hasidic *rebbe*. After many requests, the father agrees to take him to the *tzaddik* but says they will turn back if any mishap shows that the trip is ill-advised. Twice they return with broken axles; on the third trip, they reach the *tzaddik*'s town only to have a merchant tell them that the *rebbe* is not pure of action, and the father and son go home. Then the son dies and appears to his father in a dream. The son is angry, and when the rabbi asks why, the son says that the *tzaddik* he wanted to visit can tell him. After the third such dream, the rabbi travels to meet the *tzaddik*. On the way he meets the merchant whom he had met earlier, who reveals himself as Samael (Satan) and says: "Your son was in the aspect of 'the [lesser] light,' and that *tzaddik* is in the aspect of 'the great light.' If they had been united, the Messiah would have come. But now that I have done away with him, you are allowed to travel."[45]

In a simple, dramatic fashion this story brings together some of the classic themes of Hasidism: the holiness of the *tzaddik* (despite the doubts of opponents of Hasidism); the close proximity of the other world (in which the dead can speak to the living in dreams); and the yearning for the Messiah, whose coming may be imminent or long delayed. From the first readers of the *Zohar*, to the Lurianic kabbalists, to the hasidic rebbes who lived on the brink of the modern age, Jewish mystics drew direct, if often blurry, connections between our world and the supernal worlds of spirit and reward. While study and devotion to God did not decline in importance, the mystics promoted an emphasis on righteous behavior in this, the lower world, as well as an urgency to perform the *mitzvot*, to gather in the holy sparks and help achieve *tikkun olam*. In this way, every good person, rich or poor, learned or uneducated, could help bring about *tikkun olam* and have a share in the World to Come.

7

Modernity:
What Do We Believe?

*"The undiscovered country from whose bourn /
No traveller returns ..."*
(William Shakespeare, Hamlet, Act III, Scene 1)

MODERNITY IS CHARACTERIZED by its faith in science as a standard by which to determine truth and possibility. In most matters, we need empirical evidence to justify our beliefs. But while science can explain much about how humankind developed, how mind and body work, and how to keep illness at bay, it has not been able to explain what happens after we die. No doctor, no researcher, no computer program has been able to tell us where our souls go, whether there are indeed places of reward or punishment for our deeds, or whether the dead can be brought back to life. Today, many people who look to science to answer their questions about the physical world still look beyond science for insight into metaphysical matters – questions about life and death – even though the answers cannot be proven.

For most of the past two centuries, embracing modernity often meant disregarding, replacing, or even repudiating certain aspects of faith. But in the latter half of the twentieth century we have seen a resurgence of interest in spiritual matters, even to the extent that some people have reclaimed ideas that their immediate forebears may have rejected out of hand as "unscientific."

This is true of the mystical themes that are the subject of this study. With the dawning of the modern age, many Jewish philosophers, theologians, and scholars voiced a profound skepticism regarding the hereafter, especially bodily resurrection; some preferred to describe the immortality of the soul as a vague promise of eternal life rather than a definable state of being. As we proceed into a postmodern age, however, more and more scholars and Jewish laypeople alike are reexamining ideas that were pushed aside in the name of modernity.

✿ THE CHALLENGE OF MODERNITY

Beginning with the scientific advances of the eighteenth century, the modern age came to mean far-reaching changes as Enlightenment ideas were applied to every aspect of society, culminating in the revolutionary introduction of democratic ideals toward the end of that century. For European Jews, these changes represented both an opportunity and a challenge. On the one hand, the Enlightenment presented an opportunity to throw off their medieval status and participate on an equal footing in society. On the other hand, the fight for civil emancipation in the emerging modern states challenged them to acculturate in ways they had not anticipated.

During the Middle Ages, most Jews lived in communities separate from their non-Jewish compatriots; they paid high taxes to the government for the right of residence and faced economic discrimination as well as religious persecution. At the same time, Jewish communities were to some extent self-governing, with rabbis instead of civil judges deciding internal matters of law.

With the advent of the Enlightenment, this state of affairs began to change. As early as the mid-eighteenth century, Jews began to seek out secular as well as religious education and to trickle into major European cities.[1] This movement to acquire secular knowledge became known as the Jewish Enlightenment or *Haskalah*, as it was called in Central and Eastern Europe, a term based on the Hebrew word for knowledge.

Meanwhile political changes in Western Europe began to affect Jewish communities more directly. Revolutionary France was the first state to grant Jews rights of citizenship equivalent to non-Jews, while at the same time insisting on curtailing the power of Jewish leaders and rabbinic courts. In the modern state, the government's position was summarized by the French Comte de Clermont-Tonnèrre, who declared to the General Assembly in 1789: "To the Jews as individuals we should grant everything. But to the Jews as a nation – nothing." The price of citizenship was therefore the end of Jewish self-government. Jews were expected to define themselves as members of a religious affiliation only, as opposed to a "people" or a "nation," so as not to be regarded as a "state within the state." Jews in neighboring Germany, not yet emancipated, began to wonder if their prayers "for a return to Zion" decreased their likelihood for German citizenship.

Because Jews were aware that their acceptance by the general community was to some degree contingent on their behaving as other citizens did, the pursuit of emancipation brought about a significant degree of acculturation and assimilation. Judah Leib Gordon, a nineteenth-century *maskil* (an adherent of *Haskalah*), counseled Jews: "Be a Jew in your home and a man in the street." In other words, in order to participate fully in society as equals, Jews had to acquire the language, dress, and education of the majority culture.

The spread of secular education and the promise of political emancipation had a number of effects on European Jewry. It sparked the establishment of schools in which boys learned secular subjects as well as Torah and Talmud, and in urban communities, schools for girls as well, initiating the first broad movement toward female education among Jews.

But the exposure to secular learning and promise of integration also had internal ramifications for the Jewish community. Did these new ideas challenge their religious beliefs? Was a synthesis between Judaism and secular knowledge possible? How far were they willing to go in modernizing their faith?

§ﾠﾠﾠRELIGIOUS RESPONSES TO MODERNITY

The most dramatic result of the Enlightenment on European (and, soon after, North American) Jewry was the establishment of different religious trends or denominations within Judaism. Seeking to incorporate Enlightenment values into Jewish worship, groups of urban German Jews founded the first synagogues of the Reform movement. One of their goals was to reshape Jewish liturgy and ritual in accordance with the rationalist principles and the assimilationist ethos of the Enlightenment.

One revolutionary change in Reform temples was the introduction of instrumental music, which had been anathema in synagogue worship since the destruction of the Second Temple in 70 C.E. German Reformers installed organs and instituted elaborate choral arrangements of liturgical music that reflected the practice in neighboring Lutheran churches. Early Reform services also added weekly sermons and prayer in the vernacular and soon began to make changes in the liturgy of the service itself.

Meanwhile, a number of nineteenth-century rabbis reacted to the changes introduced by the Reformers, and their reactions in turn resulted in denominational splits. For example, Zachariah Frankel opposed the Reformers in defending the importance of maintaining Hebrew as the language of prayer. His followers founded the "Historical-Positive" approach to Judaism, a precursor of the Conservative movement. Samson Raphael Hirsch, a spokesman for "Neo-Orthodoxy" (known today as Modern Orthodoxy), formulated a philosophy for observant German Jews that focused on being faithful to Jewish tradition in daily life while studying and working in the modern world. Hirsch's ideal was the *yisrael mensch*, meaning a person who is fully a Jew in public and private and also a cultured individual who could mix with non-Jews in society. His agenda for Modern Orthodoxy is based on a sentence in *Pirke Avot* (Ethics of the Fathers 2:2): *Yafeh talmud Torah im derekh eretz*, "Excellent is the study of Torah with worldly knowledge." (In the twentieth century, Joseph Soloveitchik, a leading American Orthodox scholar and *rosh yeshivah* of Yeshiva University, coined a variation of this sentiment in the expression *Torah u-mada,* "Torah and science," which he viewed as a synthesis of Torah study and knowledge of Western culture.)

By the 1840s, the Reform movement in Germany was beginning to pull away from the idea of resurrection in favor of an emphasis on the immortality of the soul. The earliest Reformers did not revise the traditional prayer book's references to the afterlife, choosing instead to omit only those prayers that could be interpreted as allegiance to another nation – those that mentioned a return to Zion and the restoration of the Temple. But in 1844, a group of German rabbis meeting at a convention in Braunschweig (Brunswick) began to move Reform Judaism toward a liturgy that expressed an approach to the afterlife that they felt was more suited to modern times.

Abraham Geiger, the leading ideologue of Reform Judaism in Germany, told the conference that some ideas that had been incorporated into Judaism "have become entirely foreign to our time ... in fact have been strongly rejected by it," adding that these concepts had taken on a "spiritual" rather than a literal meaning. Geiger gave the example of the hope for an afterlife, which he said "should not be expressed in terms which suggest a future revival, a resurrection of the body; rather they must stress the immortality of the human soul."[2] In his 1854 prayer book, Geiger retained the traditional Hebrew in the second paragraph of the *Amidah* for the phrase *mehayeh ha-metim* ("God ... who revives the dead," an expression generally taken as a reference to resurrection) but he translated the passage in German as "who bestows life here and there."[3]

In the United States, the Reform liturgy went through the most radical changes. At a conference in 1869 held in Philadelphia, American Reform rabbis declared, "The belief in the bodily resurrection has no religious foundation." This assessment was reaffirmed by the fledgling Union of American Hebrew Congregations in the Pittsburgh Platform of 1885:

> We reassert the doctrine of Judaism that the soul is immortal, grounding the belief on the divine nature of human spirit, which forever finds bliss in righteousness and misery in wickedness.

> We reject as ideas not rooted in Judaism, the beliefs
> both in bodily resurrection and in Gehenna and Eden
> (Hell and Paradise) as abodes for everlasting punishment
> and reward.

Accordingly, Reform rabbis in America changed the liturgy to reflect their rejection of the doctrine of resurrection. As early as 1856, German-born Rabbi David Einhorn, leader of the "radical" wing of the Reform movement, had produced a prayer book that replaced references to resurrection with praise to God, in Hebrew and German, for "implanting within us eternal life." This wording was adopted for Reform's first move-ment-wide prayer book in Hebrew and English, *The Union Prayer Book*, in 1895, which was used in Reform services for the next eighty years.

In 1975, the new Reform prayer book, *Gates of Prayer*, replaced the traditional Hebrew benediction *mehayeh ha-metim* ("who revives the dead") with *mehayeh ha-kol* ("who gives life to all"). Prayer books of the Reconstructionist movement, the first of which appeared in 1945, use similar phrasing in accordance with the naturalistic philosophy of the founder of Reconstructionism, Rabbi Mordecai M. Kaplan.[4]

The Conservative movement, which grew out of the establishment of The Jewish Theological Seminary in New York in 1887, has consistently maintained the traditional Hebrew phrase *mehayeh ha-metim* in its prayer books, but, as Rabbi Neil Gillman says, "shades the English translation to reflect a more modern sensibility."[5] For example, the Conservative movement's 1985 prayer book, *Siddur Sim Shalom*, translates *mehayeh ha-metim* as "master of life and death." Its predecessor, the prayer book edited by Rabbi Morris Silverman, translated the same phrase as "who callest the dead to life everlasting."

In its statement of principles, a pamphlet titled *Emet v'Emunah* first issued in 1988, the United Synagogue of Conservative Judaism affirmed the doctrine of bodily resurrection, although it allowed that individuals could understand traditional teachings in various ways, some view-ing them as literal truth, others treating them more as metaphor. "The doctrine of the resurrection of the dead," the statement reads, "affirms in a striking way the value Judaism accords to our bodily existence in our concrete historical and social setting."6

No such shading is used in vernacular translations of *siddurim* (prayer books) used by Orthodox Jews, which to this day praise the Eternal as the One who "revives the dead," "resurrects the dead," "resuscitates the dead," or "quickens the dead." Samson Raphael Hirsch, who left a translation and commentary of the traditional *siddur* in manuscript form at the time of his death in 1888, remarked in his commentary on the *Gevurot* prayer,

> There can hardly be another thought that can so inspire man firmly to resolve to live a life so vigorous, unwavering, fearless and unswervingly dutiful than the belief in *tehiyat ha-metim* [the revival of the dead]. This is the firm conviction that to God not even the dead are lost forever, and that, even for the physical body, death is not the end but only a transition period from one life to the next.7

Accordingly, traditional prayer books, in the prayer praising God's powers, continue to affirm the promise made when Isaiah proclaimed that the dead would arise and shout for joy (Isaiah 26:19) and Daniel foresaw a time when "many of those who sleep in the dust of the earth will awake" (Daniel 12:2). The Artscroll *siddur*, for example, translates *mehayeh ha-metim* as "the resuscitator of the dead" and posits that the phrase refers to

> ... three kinds of resuscitation: man's awakening every morning after deathlike slumber; the rain that has the life-sustaining quality of making vegetation grow; and the literal resuscitation of the dead that will take place in the messianic age.8

The tension between what modern Jews know of science and what they believe about God's powers is acknowledged but dismissed by

Rabbi J. H. Hertz (1872–1946), the late Chief Rabbi of Great Britain, in his *siddur* commentary:

> Many people find Resurrection incredible; yet it is not more of a mystery than birth, or the stupendous miracle of the annual resurrection of plant-life after winter.[9]

This comment affirms that even in an age ruled by science, many Jews have been able to keep faith with the traditional promise of bodily resurrection. To this day, some Jews wish to be buried on the Mount of Olives in Jerusalem, which is where, according to the Jerusalem Talmud, resurrection will begin when the Messiah comes.[10]

✿ RECLAIMING OUR SPIRITUAL LIVES

With World War II and its attendant horrors – the Holocaust in Europe and the destruction of urban centers in Europe and Asia through firebombing and the first use of atomic weapons – came a sense that knowledge and science, the backbone of modernity, were not enough to ensure a civilized world. For Jews, stunned by the crimes of the Nazis and their collaborators, the shock and the disillusionment were especially severe.

Postmodernism, the collection of ideas that question modernity's confidence in science and technology as tools to solve all the problems of humankind, did not become a catchword until the 1980s, but its influence was apparent well ahead of that time. Writers and thinkers, right after the war, began to question the values of a culture that could not prevent the horrors of the twentieth century. Moreover, as the first postwar generation came of age in the 1960s and 1970s, many young people challenged not only their governments and societal values but also the religious traditions in which they had been raised. It was at this time that large numbers of young Jews began to explore religious traditions outside Judaism, such as Eastern religions, or to embrace Orthodoxy as *ba'alei teshuvah* (newly observant Jews), looking to traditional Judaism for a more "spiritual" experience than they had known as children.

Other Jews of the baby-boomer generation sought a more intimate, emotionally compelling form of Judaism. In the 1970s, the *havurah* movement began with small groups of young Jews that met for worship services and to study Jewish texts together. This "grassroots" model for discovering Judaism led to a proliferation of small, informal congregations and, in larger synagogues, to the creation of smaller affinity groups and "alternative" services.

Some Jews have turned to a kind of neo-Hasidism in their worship style, incorporating joyous song and dance into services. Neo-Hasidism has had a significant influence on mainstream North American Judaism, infusing it with spiritual meaning through music and mysticism, folk traditions based on Eastern European customs, and stories from classic Yiddish sources. Contemporary Jews in search of a more direct spiritual experience also have incorporated practices such as meditation into their worship and have created or updated many rituals celebrating the human life cycle.

In time, the quest for heightened spirituality among mainstream Jews merged with the desire to address questions that science and other received wisdom could not answer, including questions about the hereafter. Speculation that might have seemed too remote or fanciful to be relevant in the early part of the twentieth century now became part of the Jewish conversation and even the focus of academic study. In recent years, Jewish scholars and theologians across the ideological spectrum have explored such topics as resurrection and reincarnation, drawing on ideas from 2,500 years of Jewish thought and, in some cases, reclaiming traditions that formerly had been pushed aside.[11]

Recently, with its newest prayer book, *Mishkan T'filah*,[12] the Reform movement has come full circle, printing the traditional *Gevurot* blessing ending with *mehayeh ha-metim* alongside the version that ends *mehayeh ha-kol* ("who gives life to all"), thereby presenting the worshiper with both options. "Not all Reform Jews believe in the afterlife, a consequence, perhaps, of our movement's confusion of uncertainty with irrationality," writes David Posner, the senior rabbi of New York's Temple Emanu-El. "Belief in the World to Come may be uncertain, but it is not irrational. After all, why would our Creator . . . consign us to oblivion?"[13]

Jon D. Levenson, professor at Harvard Divinity School, also urges a new look at resurrection from a theological perspective:

> Whether in the vision of national restoration in Ezekiel 37, the ambiguous revival of the dead in Isaiah 26, or the clear prediction of resurrection with judgment in Daniel 12, resurrection does not simply vindicate the justice of God. It also fulfills the promise to Israel of the God of life. And in that, all these texts in their differing ways adumbrate the affirmation that the ancient rabbis ordained that Jews must make every day of their lives – the affirmation that God "keeps faith with those who sleep in the dust."[14]

So an era that began with a rush to embrace knowledge of the world as the solution to all problems has given way to a time in which educated people, enjoying worldly pleasures, can still believe that death is not the end of life and that a World to Come may be real even if it is not provable. Certainly this postmodern sensibility is rooted in the understanding that scientific knowledge alone does not end hatred, persecution, and lunacy on a global scale. Perhaps it is also informed by technology, which, through its ability to measure God's universe, reminds of us of its infinity. The sheer scope of the twentieth century's scientific breakthroughs is more prone to generate awe than overconfidence, forcing us to acknowledge that there remain phenomena that are beyond our understanding. Therefore, it is precisely to our faith traditions that we still turn for insights on the mysteries of life and death.

I. L. Peretz (1852–1915), the secular, Warsaw-based Yiddish writer who loved all things Jewish, could have told us this. In one of his most famous stories, "Three Gifts,"[15] the soul of a departed Jew cannot be sent to either heaven or hell because his good deeds and bad are perfectly balanced on the scales of the Heavenly Court. Taking pity on the poor soul, which is doomed to wander between heaven and earth, an angel advises him to find three gifts with which to bribe the saints in Paradise to admit him (in Peretz's stories, saints can be bribed). As the soul flies over the world of the living, one of the "gifts" he finds is the following deed: A wealthy Jew in the midst of being robbed is willing to relinquish all his earthly possessions except one for which he is ready to fight to the death: a small bag of earth from the Holy Land. He had been saving this bag of earth for his burial so that he might be closer to the Land of Israel when the Messiah comes to resurrect the dead. The man is willing to give up everything but his share in the World to Come – and I. L. Peretz regards that belief as a great gift.

The Messiah: The Eternal Thread of Hope

> ⚘ On the day the Temple was destroyed, the Messiah
> was born. (*Lamentations Rabbah 1:51*)

BELIEF IN THE eventual arrival of a Messiah and a messianic age refers most readily to an eschatology relating to this world: God will send the Messiah who arrives in a time of disaster and havoc and initiates an era of faith, righteousness, and peace. But the Messiah is also a bridge to the next world in that his arrival will put into motion the process of redemption that will unlock the gates to the World to Come. This otherworldly view of the Messiah shifts and evolves over three thousand years of Jewish history, depending on historical circumstances, theology, and philosophy. Influenced by the biblical prophets, the idea of the Messiah teaches that history is advancing toward a purpose that will take humanity in a different and better direction.

There are differing opinions about whether the Messiah's arrival will have more impact on this world or the next, the World to Come. However, the belief in a Messiah is a basic expression of the Jewish spirit that has helped Jews to endure times of suffering throughout the ages. It is permeated with an aura of ultimate hope and redemption for Israel and for humanity. In this chapter, we will trace the development of ideas about the Messiah as well as messianic movements that these ideas inspired.

✿   BIBLICAL ORIGINS OF THE MESSIAH

The English word "Messiah," translated from the Hebrew *mashiah,* meaning "anointed one," is derived from the ancient Hebrew practice of anointing with oil any person charged with a divine office, such as a king or priest. Among the many leaders so anointed was King David, and to this day many Jews believe that the Messiah will derive from the Davidic line of descent.

In the time of the kings and prophets, from about the eighth century B.C.E. until the destruction of the First Temple in 586 B.C.E., the hope of salvation began to play a dominant and conspicuous role in the life of the people. This led to an extension of the term "Messiah" to carry the idea that the anointed individual had the power to save and redeem. Therefore, in the Jewish imagination, the Davidic persona and era gradually came to be used as the blueprint for an imagined future Messiah and messianic age, in which a divinely inspired king would arrive during a period of war, evildoing, and social iniquity to restore peace and righteousness.

In the Bible we have the antecedents for the image of the Messiah figure. The future age is described as a time of unparalleled plenty and spiritual tranquillity. One example is the well-known passage from Isaiah, which in its first line refers to David's father, Jesse, and to David as "branch from his roots":

There shall come forth a stalk from the stock of Jesse

> And a branch from his roots shall bear fruit
> And the spirit of the Lord shall rest upon him . . . .
> And he shall strike the earth with the rod of his mouth
> And with the breath of his lips he shall slay the wicked. . . .
> For the earth shall be filled with the knowledge of God
> As the waters cover the sea.   (Isaiah 11:1–9)

Preaching in the eighth century B.C.E., Amos and other prophets describe a period of affliction and harsh judgment as punishment for the Hebrews' sins; Amos refers to this time as *Yom Adonai*, the "Day of the Lord."[1] But it is also God, Amos says, who will gather back the scattered people to their land and will restore their independence and prosperity in an era of peace.[2] Later prophets such as Nahum, Zephaniah, Habak-kuk, Joel, and Malachi refer to God, not a human figure, as the redeemer.

The prophets Isaiah, Micah, Jeremiah, and Zechariah, however, set forth a redeeming figure separate from God: an ideal human leader pos-sessed of lofty spiritual and ethical qualities. The last of the prophets, Malachi, introduces the concept of the prophet Elijah as the harbinger of the Messiah's arrival, based on Elijah's having been taken to heaven in God's chariot rather than dying: "I will send the prophet Elijah to you before the great and awesome day of the Lord" (Malachi 3:23). This idea, which captured the Jewish imagination, echoes to this day in Jewish ritual and theology.[3] For the rabbis of the talmudic period, Elijah loomed large as a herald of the Messiah and was even involved in the resurrection of the dead.

Although the visions of the prophets are not consistent, we can assemble a scenario for the coming of the messianic age through their pronouncements. It would look something like this:

- God levels a great judgment upon the wicked world
- The Day of the Lord arrives; the wicked are punished
- Israel is established in its land under the rule of a righteous king
- The nations of the world recognize the God of Israel
- Justice, righteousness, and peace spread throughout the world

In forecasting the future, the biblical prophets posit a human redeemer who will usher in a utopian future based in part on visions of a past Golden Age.

THE MESSIAH IN SECOND TEMPLE WRITINGS

While the Apocrypha contains no mention of the Messiah, several of the books in the Pseudepigrapha contain significant messianic material that also connects to the subject of the hereafter.[4] Most relevant to our discussion are the books ascribed to Enoch, which present a heavenly and transcendent principal figure whom God has designated as the one who will judge at the end of days, vindicating the righteous and the elect and eventually bringing about their resurrection. The text refers to this heavenly being as the "Chosen One," the "Son of Man," and "God's Anointed." Enoch asks his informant, an angel, to explain who this mysterious figure is. The angel answers:

> This is the Son of Man to whom belongs righteousness and with whom righteousness dwells. And he will open up all the hidden storerooms, for the Lord of the spirits has chosen him, and he is destined to be victorious before the Lord of the spirits in eternal uprightness. This one will remove the kings and the mighty ones from their comfortable seats and the strong ones from their thrones.
> (1 Enoch 46:3–4).[5]

Within the book as a whole, however, the identity of the Messiah is somewhat ambiguous. In some verses, God does the judging, but in others, the Son of Man is the judge. In later passages, Enoch himself appears to be the individual who will usher in the era of peace for the righteous.[6] Elsewhere, Enoch asserts that on the Day of Judgment, four angels – Michael, Gabriel, Raphael, and Phanuel – will mete out punishment to the wicked. Wisdom will be given to the elect, among whom is the Messiah, and they will live and never sin again.

The Second Book of Enoch, like the First, is a revelation of apocalypse, which describes the end of the world and the workings of heaven and hell. It includes one of the first enumerations of seven heavens and an early description of Paradise that links Eden with a heavenly afterlife for those who are worthy. Enoch also appears in a third pseudepigraphical book that carries his name. This book, which borrows more heavily from rabbinic rather than from priestly thinking, describes the process of mystical ascent and discusses the transmigration of souls.[7]

Other pseudepigraphical writings reflect the political realities of the time and their influence on Jewish thinking. For example, one of the Psalms of Solomon, which comprise the response of a group of pious Jews to the capture of Jerusalem by Romans in the first century B.C.E., extols the reign of the hoped-for king, the anointed son of David, who will deliver the Jews from oppression. Similarly, 4 Ezra describes the arrival of the Messiah, with final judgment and resurrection taking place after a series of upheavals.

In these writings, we see two different visions of the Messiah: one of Messiah as king, a political figure who will solve the social and economic problems suffered by an oppressed nation, and the other of a transcendent figure, a Chosen One who possesses the powers of a more-than-human judge and who will usher in an age of peace and prosperity. We can also see the tension between the two visions, as well as the foundation for the Christian view of the Messiah in the second vision, in which the Messiah becomes an incarnation of God. The point of interest in Jewish thought is the idea that the coming of the messianic age follows a definite scenario, an idea that later rabbinic tradition describes and develops.

THE MESSIAH IN RABBINIC LITERATURE

Given the practical and legal nature of most of the Mishnah, it is understandable that it contains only two references to the Messiah. Nevertheless, it is still puzzling in contrast to the Mishnah's thirty references to the World to Come. Why doesn't the rabbis' vision of the World to Come include the arrival of the Messiah?

One of the two references, in *Berakhot* 1:5, is a passing mention, but the other, at the end of Mishnah *Sotah*, describes the death of one sage after another, a gradual draining of wisdom, learning, and goodness from the world, leading to a time of greatest darkness that immediately precedes the Messiah's arrival.

This text, *Sotah* 9:15, sometimes called "the little apocalypse," is unique in the Mishnah as it depicts the social and political upheavals, famines, epidemics, and economic deprivations caused by apostasy, desecration of God's name, and willful ignorance of the Torah. However, as one of the sages points out, humanity can be saved by attaining ascending levels of personal sanctity. Here, as in Malachi, the prophet Elijah is named as the herald of the messianic age:

> With the footsteps of the Messiah, arrogance shall increase and dearth reach its peak. . . . Truth shall nowhere be found. The young will insult the old, the son will dishonor the father, the daughter the mother. . . .
>
> R. Pinhas b. Yair says . . . the shunning of sin leads to saintliness, and saintliness leads to [the gift of] the Holy Spirit, and the Holy Spirit leads to the resurrection of the dead, and the resurrection of the dead shall come through Elijah of blessed memory.

This apocalyptic language, as well as the paucity of references to the Messiah, makes sense given the circumstances under which Palestinian Jews lived during the second century. Still traumatized from the destruction of the Temple, and later by the Bar Kokhba revolt of 132–135 C.E., which ended in utter defeat, many Jews were drawn to the idea of messianic salvation. This created a precarious situation for the codifiers of the Mishnah, who had to maintain the Jewish people's hope for the future but could not afford to anger the Roman occupiers, whose rule had become increasingly hostile not only to Jewish political autonomy but to Jewish study and practice as well. The oppression reached its height in the Romans' brutal response to the Bar Kokhba revolt. Although it would seem that the idea of a personal redeemer would be especially attractive to the sages during such dark times, they apparently felt it prudent to leave the question of the Messiah's identity and role to future generations. Indeed, among all the sages of the mishnaic period, only Rabbi Akiva identified a specific candidate for Messiah, declaring, as recorded in the Jerusalem Talmud, that Bar Kokhba himself would attain that status.[8]

By contrast, the Talmud, compiled by rabbis in those future generations who lived and taught in the academies of Palestine and Babylonia, has scores of references to the Messiah and the messianic age. The question that preoccupied the sages of the Talmud was: when will the Messiah come? What actions – historical, social, and religious – will bring him? Having learned from the Bar Kokhba tragedy, they veer away from the political into the spiritual. The *amoraim,* the sages of the Talmud, never propose any practical or political steps that will bring the Messiah, as Rabbi Akiva had. Rather, we hear a great deal in the Talmud about the Messiah's personal qualities of mind and soul. The rabbis describe a Messiah with such finely honed spiritual powers that he will be able to tell by smell alone who is wicked and who is righteous. They present a Messiah who is of this world, but whose task is to prepare humankind for the next world, for resurrection, and the World to Come.

The *amoraim* loved to talk about the coming of Messiah and to speculate on the details of his arrival. Many *aggadot,* or legends, recounted in the Talmud describe the Messiah's presence at the gates of the city and his entrance among the people. For example, a passage in *Sanhedrin* 98a shows the prophet Elijah visiting one of the rabbis and telling the rabbi where the Messiah can be found:

> R. Joshua b. Levi met Elijah standing by the entrance of R. Simeon b. Yohai's tomb. He asked him: "Have I a portion in the World to Come?"
>
> He replied, "If this Master desires it."
>
> R. Joshua b. Levi said, "I saw two, but heard the voice of a third [the voice of the Shekhinah]." He then asked [Elijah], "When will the Messiah come?"
>
> "Go and ask him himself," was his reply.
>
> "Where is he sitting?"
>
> "At the entrance [of the city]."

The rabbi then goes to meet the Messiah, who is sitting among the poor and oppressed and rebandaging the wounds of lepers, and reports back to Elijah that the Messiah told him he would arrive that day, which Elijah interprets as a promise to the rabbi that he will have a share in the World to Come – the answer to the rabbi's original question.

A survey of talmudic discussions about the Messiah reveals a new, more detailed chronology for the events leading to his arrival:

- The world becomes progressively worse
- There is bitter warfare between nations[9]
- Famine, pestilence, and earthquakes strike the world
- God sends the Messiah (heralded by Elijah) to intervene and resolve worldly strife
- The Messiah destroys enemy nations
- The dead are resurrected and reunited with their souls
- The righteous will enjoy the World to Come

Yet among the *amoraim,* we hear differing views on whether the Messiah is of this world or the next, a debate that has continued through the centuries. Rabbi Samuel, a third-century Babylonian teacher, has a somewhat naturalistic, political view of the messianic age:

> There is no difference between this world and the days of the Messiah except [that in the latter there will be no] bondage of foreign powers.   (*Berakhot* 34b)

By contrast, Rabbi Yohanan, in the same passage, puts forth an other-worldly view:

> All the prophets prophesied only for the days of the Messiah, but as for the World to Come, 'Eye hath not seen, O God, beside thee.'

Rabbi Yohanan's view of the Messiah is more mystical, suggesting that he is an omen of, rather than an actor helping to bring about, the World to Come and all its mysteries. According to Rabbi Yohanan, while the Messiah will usher in the miraculous age of the World to Come, only God knows what it will look like.[10]

Though it was frowned upon, some talmudic rabbis could not resist attempting to calculate when the Messiah would come,[11] a practice known as "reckoning the end":

> Cursed be they who calculate "the end," because they argue that since "the end" has arrived and the Messiah has not come, he never will come. But wait for him [nevertheless], as it is written, "Though he tarry, wait for him." (*Sanhedrin* 97b)

We also find a number of talmudic rabbis adopting the idea of a messianic age that will serve as a bridge between this world and the next and will last a specific number of years. For example, in *Sanhedrin* 99a, Rabbi Eliezer holds that it will last for forty years (the period the Israelites spent in the desert); Rabbi Dosa, four hundred years (the period of the Israelites' sojourn in Egypt); and Rabbi Yehuda Ha-Nasi, three hundred and sixty-five years (reflecting the number of days in a year), with other rabbis foreseeing longer terms.[12] Many rabbis believed that the period of the Messiah ("the Days of the Messiah") would be only a transition stage between this world and the World to Come.

Finally, the rabbis discussed at length the behavior required to bring the Messiah. That arrival, they stressed, is incumbent upon Jews upholding their moral standards and ritual commitments:

> All "the ends" have passed and still the Messiah has not come; it depends only upon repentance and good deeds. (BT *Sanhedrin* 97b)

> If [the whole of] Israel [genuinely] repented a single day, the son of David would come immediately. If [the whole of] Israel observed a single Sabbath properly, the son of David would come immediately. (JT *Ta'anit* 64a)

> If Israel were to keep two [consecutive] Sabbaths accord-
> ing to the law, they would be redeemed forthwith.
>
> (BT *Shabbat* 118b)

Because they describe a uniformity of devotion and behavior that is difficult if not impossible to attain, these passages show the lengths to which Jews as a community must go to attract the Messiah, as does this statement from Rabbi Yohanan: "The son of David will come only in a generation that is either altogether righteous or altogether wicked."[13]

THE MESSIAH IN THE MIDDLE AGES

The doctrine of the Messiah was codified by Maimonides into one of his "Thirteen Principles" of the Jewish faith:

> I believe with perfect faith in the coming of the Messiah:
> even if he tarry, I will still believe and wait every day for
> him . . . .
>
> (Introduction to his commentary on the Mishnah)

Having said this, however, Maimonides had to explain his understanding of the messianic age. He saw the references to the marvels of the messianic age in the Bible, such as Isaiah's vision of the wolf lying together with the lamb, not as literal predictions but as metaphors for an Israel living at peace among the other nations of the world, which for their part will have embraced Judaism and therefore will have ceased to persecute Israel. The Messiah will be an ordinary human being who will teach the word of God to all people, but no miracle-worker, according to Maimonides:

> Do not think that the King Messiah will have to perform
> signs and wonders, bring anything new into being,
> revive the dead or do similar things. It is not so. . . . He

will prepare the whole world to serve the Lord with one accord, as it is written: "For then will I make the people pure of speech, that they may all call upon the name of the Lord to serve Him with one consent."[14]

Nor will the coming of the messianic age mean any fundamental change in the world God created:

Let no one think that in the days of the Messiah any of the laws of nature will be set aside, or any innovation be introduced into creation. The world will follow its normal course.[15]

Although the Messiah that Maimonides envisioned was a mortal human being, he was certainly a paragon among men: he would be a king of Davidic descent, a Torah scholar, a keeper of the commandments, an effective preacher, and a warrior for God. Upon his death, the Messiah would be succeeded by his son, also a king, and under the son's rule, the Jews would be relieved of many of their current troubles and would be able to devote themselves more thoroughly to spiritual matters.

The extent to which Maimonides demystifies the Messiah is striking, but his view sits well within the tradition of the rabbis as well as being consistent with his rationalist bent. It is certainly a contrast to the Christian idea that the Messiah is an incarnation of God with supernatural powers. While the Jewish Messiah had glimmers of supernatural elements, he was entirely human. At the same time, there is no conflict between Maimonides' naturalistic description of the Messiah and his supernatural vision of an afterlife in which righteous people attain spiritual perfection, have no need for physical accoutrements, and are warmed in the radiance of God's presence.

Although Nahmanides' views on the afterlife were of a more mystical turn than those of Maimonides, his ideas concerning the Messiah's identity were similar. During a 1263 disputation, Nahmanides defended Jewish doctrine against the arguments of an apostate Jew who had converted to Christianity. He asserted, in opposition to the Christian view of a divine Messiah, that the prophets regarded the Messiah as human and that he had not yet arrived on Earth. Moreover, Nahmanides argued that the prophets had also promised that the messianic era would be one of peace and universal justice, yet the world was still filled with violence since the appearance of Jesus.[16]

THE MESSIAH IN JEWISH MYSTICISM

The mystics presented a complex and variable concept of the Messiah and more readily embraced the supernatural aspects of the Messiah and the messianic age. They concerned themselves not only with the Messiah's powers and identity, but also with the source and content of his soul.

Theories about the Messiah's soul vary, but mystical thinkers did largely agree that it would come from the highest reaches of cosmic reality and, while of elevated quality, would be a human soul. The various kabbalistic schools were not in agreement about whether the Messiah's soul would be subject to transmigration or reincarnation. Some believed that it is the soul of Adam, which migrated to King David,[17] and associated the Messiah with the *sefirah* called *malkhut,* kingdom.[18]Although the main body of the Zohar, the first important kabbalistic work, does not mention the Messiah very much, it contains apocalyptic passages and even hints about when the Messiah will arrive. In messianic terms, Rabbi Shimon bar Yohai, to whom the Zohar is attributed, was seen as "a spark of Moses," someone in whom Moses' soul had been reincarnated. As Arthur Green, a contemporary scholar of Jewish mysticism, writes: "It is clear that in the *Idrot* [sections of the Zohar] the Zohar's central hero [Rabbi Shimon] has made a transition from the archetype of *tzaddik* to something very like a messianic or proto-messianic figure."[19]

Likewise, in the sixteenth century, Isaac Luria's disciples saw Luria as inheritor of Rabbi Shimon's soul and messianic purpose, along with the ability to nourish the souls of humanity and bring about *tikkun olam,* the repair of the world. The writings of Luria's followers, such as Hayyim Vital, clearly portray Luria as the redeemer of his generation. Lurianic kabbalists shifted the focus from the utopian to the practical; instead of awaiting an ideal end of days, it is the duty of humanity to carry out repair – in kabbalistic terms, to gather up the sparks – and make the world fit to receive the Messiah. Such a view dovetails with the readiness of Jews to seek redeemers at a time when persecution of Jews was frequent and widespread.

Perhaps the most significant impact of the willingness to believe in the Messiah's imminent arrival is the ease with which it allowed false messiahs to flourish. The most notorious of these was Shabbetai Tzvi (1626–1676) who claimed to be the Messiah and attracted a large following among Jews throughout Europe. Because of his activities, Tzvi was arrested and imprisoned by the Ottoman authorities. Given the choice of converting to Islam or being put to death, he chose Islam, crushing the hopes of almost all his followers. Other messianic pretenders arose afterwards with similarly disappointing results.

Despite the "false Messiah" debacle, the generation of Jews after Shabbetai Tzvi continued to embrace the idea of the Messiah, but in a different form. Hasidism channeled their longing for a personal Messiah into allegiance to *tzaddikim* ("righteous ones"), local rabbis of demonstrated wisdom and saintliness who became exemplars of messianic values and who commanded the devotion of their followers. In this way, the mystical trends of Kabbalah flowed into hasidic teachings, bringing a Lurianic agenda to instructions for daily behavior that would eventually bring about the messianic age and would eventually enable the dead to be resurrected and the righteous to enter the World to Come.

MESSIANISM AND MODERNITY

The modern age has seen a divergence between Liberal and Orthodox theologians on the subject of the Messiah. It is intriguing, however, that very few have been prepared to abandon the doctrine entirely. Instead, it has served as a springboard for the expression of various aspirations.

In the era of the Enlightenment, the hopes of many Western and Central European Jews were based on their own aspirations for the spread of liberalism, culture, and improvement of the human as well as the Jewish condition. As we have seen in the previous chapter, theologians of what is now called Classical Reform Judaism were eager to jettison the notion of a personal Messiah and bodily resurrection, along with prayers for returning to Zion and rebuilding the Temple in Jerusalem. They preferred to speak about a messianic age, which they defined as a future of universal peace and justice.

The early twentieth century saw the emergence of secular Jews who no longer defined their messianism in religious terms, but were eager to join secular movements for changing and redeeming the world. It is fair to say that in the modern era, the messianic impulse remained strong though the form and content had changed. But perhaps the most significant change was in the underlying attitude concerning human initiative in changing the world.

Rabbi Eugene Borowitz, a leading Reform philosopher, summarizes the Jewish modernist view of the messianic age when he cites Zionism as an example of humans taking responsibility for their own destinies:

> Our modern sense of our spiritual capacity and the resulting worth that inheres in us require us to claim a more active role in our relationship with God, Zionism being the classic example. We cannot any longer see the religious legitimacy of limiting our action to waiting for the Messiah to bring us back to the land of Israel. We believe in taking more personal responsibility for our destiny than our traditionalist forebears did, so we pursue politics as well as *mitzvot* [commandments.][20]

Secular political Zionism is a version of messianism, which adopted elements in the Jewish messianic tradition concerning efforts to restore the Jews to their ancient homeland. Even the founders of political Zionism, which originated in Western Europe in the wake of the Enlightenment, did not look upon Zionism as mere nationalism but always implied that they were fulfilling the prophetic vision that the Jews would one day return to their land. Thus their movement was a continuation, in secular terms, of a Jewish messianic hope.

The Zionist movement began as a secular attempt to address the persistence of anti-Semitism in post-Enlightenment Europe by reestablishing Jews in their own state as "a nation among nations." In many cases, early Zionists, especially in Eastern Europe, were rebels against the religious traditionalism of their elders, or at least against what they perceived as the quietism of that tradition.

Throughout the modern era, belief in a personal Messiah sent by God remained a tenet of Orthodox Judaism. Part of the faith of traditional Jews was a willingness to wait for God's redemption. The failure of Bar Kokhba's revolt in the second century had taught them of dangers of changing their destiny by physical force. The enormous disappointment following Shabbetai Tzvi's apostasy taught them to be wary of declaring false messiahs. But more than anything, traditional Jews clung to their faith that God would redeem them in His time, even when they felt they could have used a redeemer sooner. From an Orthodox religious perspective, the Zionist enterprise – to gather the Jews in Zion and reestablish their state there – seemed an audacious attempt to bring the Messiah and forcibly hasten the redemption.

Some Orthodox thinkers in the late nineteenth century were also Zionists. They continued to believe in the coming of a personal Messiah, and also believed in a return to the Land of Israel. The Polish rabbi Tzvi Hirsch Kalischer (1795–1874) and the Bosnian-born Rabbi Yehudah Alkalai (1798–1878) were two of the earliest exponents of religious Zionism. Kalischer believed that the redemption would begin not with the sudden appearance of the Messiah to lead Jews to Israel, but by Jews' own wish to settle there.[21]

The most prominent among the religious Zionist leaders was Rabbi Avraham Yitzhak Kook (1865–1935), the first Chief Rabbi of Palestine. Kook, a Lithuanian Jew who immigrated to Palestine in 1904, was deeply inspired by the work of the pioneers, whom he regarded as instruments of God's plan for salvation despite their irreligious behavior. He was a mystic who saw external events as symbols of deeper hidden reality, and so to him, the pioneers' actions were part of the cosmic process of restoring harmony to a fragmented world. Consequently, he understood the secular approach of the Zionists as part of a greater providential design to quicken the conclusion of history with the return of the Jews to their ancient homeland.

Zionism took on a new urgency in the years immediately after the Holocaust when desperate survivors became homeless refugees with no place to go. For many, Israel was their only hope, physically and spiritually. When Israel declared its statehood in 1948 and prevailed in a war against its enemies, Jews around the world experienced it as something of a miracle. The elation that they felt over the reality of a Jewish homeland in Zion after two thousand years of exile gave Israel's existence a spiritual cast. Israel's ability to provide a home for Jewish refugees and communities from many lands were triumphs that seemed almost miraculous in scope.

Nevertheless, Zionism still had its detractors among religious traditionalists. The establishment of the State of Israel and the phenomenon of secular Zionism has presented an ideological and theological problem for ultra-Orthodox and hasidic Jews. On the one hand, the presence of Jews as a people once again living in the land of their ancestors was well established by 1948. On the other hand, the view that the coming of the Messiah is miraculous and therefore cannot be hastened by human effort remains a guiding tenet for many religious Jews. The most vocal opponent of modern Zionism and the Jewish state in the postwar years was the Satmar Rebbe, Joel Teitelbaum (1887–1979), who argued that Jews should not attempt to bring about the redemption on a national level but instead accept their suffering and wait for miraculous redemption by the Messiah.[22]

In response to the Satmar Rebbe, Rabbi Aaron Soloveitchik (1922–2001), a modern Orthodox scholar, claimed that redemption could come in two different forms. The first, the *ketz nigleh* or "revealed end," is a paradigm of history and natural process. The second, the *ketz nistar*, or "hidden end," is miraculous and supernatural. If the Jews did not repent (repentance in this case meaning a return to Orthodox observance), then redemption would take place on a natural level, but slowly.[23] Conversely, if the Jews did repent, the Messiah would come miraculously, as suggested by the image of the Messiah riding in on the clouds in Daniel 7:13. Rabbi Soloveitchik also held that after the Holocaust, the Jews could regard themselves as released from any oath not to return to the land by force.[24]

Another religious response – opposite to the Satmar's rejection of Israel – is a militant strain of religious Zionism that appeared after the Six-Day War. Rabbi Tzvi Yehuda Kook, son of former Chief Rabbi Avraham Yitzhak Kook, formed the political movement *Gush Emunim* ("Bloc of the Faithful"), which spearheaded the campaign to establish Jewish settlements on land conquered during the 1967 war. To Kook and his followers, maintaining Jewish control of all the land described in the Bible as God's gift to the Israelites is an article of faith – a crucial step toward bringing the Messiah.

Most religious Zionists today espouse some kind of middle position that confirms the special status of the State of Israel as the beginning of the redemption but at the same time allows for the fact that the modern state does not possess the utopian qualities or the potential for prophetic fulfillment associated with the Messiah and the messianic age.

Finally, followers of the Chabad-Lubavitch sect of Hasidism believe that the age of redemption is imminent – with Israel's ingathering of Jews from the former Communist states and Arab lands and Israel's victory in the 1967 war, which restored the biblical patrimony. Lubavitcher *hasidim* believe that now the Messiah will come when the majority of Jews return to religious observance. The Lubavitcher *rebbe*, Menachem Mendel Schneerson, had said: "[This] generation is the last generation of Exile and the first generation of Redemption."[25] Some Lubavitcher *hasidim* believe that the Rebbe, who died in 1994, was the Messiah and that he will return.

Despite the profound differences in the ways that Jews view the Messiah and messianic age in our times, most Jewish movements and individual Jews draw on the idea that the responsibility for taking the first steps in perfecting the world lies with human beings. The idea that correction, repair, and redemption are possible and achievable is a powerful one both theologically and psychologically. As modern events have shown us, repair of the world is dependent on collective action. Accordingly, one of the meanings of *tikkun olam* in our own times is making the world a place that the Messiah will want to enter in order to complete the redemption of humankind.

The Jewish belief in the Messiah and the promise of a messianic age, as we have seen, runs like a thread of hope throughout Jewish history. From generation to generation, this messianic hope reflects the enduring Jewish faith in the vision of a redemptive future.

Afterword

WHAT, THEN, DO Jews believe about the afterlife? As we have seen, Jewish tradition has not one answer but many. Taken together, Jewish ideas about the afterlife comprise a vision of human perfectibility and divine protection.

These ideas can be summarized as follows:

- *Resurrection:* The idea that a person's body will be awakened from death and reunited with its soul in the messianic age is a basic Jewish concept, rooted in biblical texts and brought to flower by the rabbinic sages. While the modern era brought some skepticism about resurrection among Jews who pulled away from strict tradition, many post-modern thinkers have re-evaluated the knee-jerk "scientific" reaction to the idea of resurrection and consider it a corollary to the idea of the soul's immortality.

- *The Immortality of the Soul:* The idea that one's soul outlives the body is widely accepted, although Jewish thinkers have proffered various interpretations of where the soul goes after the body dies. The soul's immortality remains an important part of Jewish doctrine to this day, as reflected in the liturgy of the morning prayers:

> My God, the soul that You have given me is pure; You created it, You formed it, You breathed it into me, and You have kept it within me. And in the future You will take it from me, but You will return it to me in the hereafter."[1]

- *Reincarnation:* Ideas about reincarnation (*gilgul*) continue to be a subject of lively discussion among modern Jews. The kabbalists of the medieval period brought this subject to the fore as a focus of Jewish scholarship and the Lurianic school of Kabbalah spread its views of reincarnation across Eastern Europe. Isaac Luria and his disciples taught that the cycles of return represent the soul's efforts to perfect itself, whether to atone for sin, to fulfill a commandment, or to complete a task left unfinished at death. This notion of the individual's perfectibility resonates with the concept of *tikkun olam,* the effort to perfect the world by doing good works.

- *The World to Come:* Since the days of the rabbis, the sages of the Mishnah and the Talmud, Judaism has remained wedded to the concept of the World to Come (*olam ha-ba*). As we have seen, this term connotes a perfect existence in a future time; sometimes it refers to the afterlife and at other times to the world that will succeed the messianic age. The essential point is that the possibility of an ideal world exists, and that possibility, to some extent, defines us as human beings. "Man is a citizen of two worlds – this world and the World to Come," Rabbi Joseph Hertz wrote in his commentary to the *Gevurot* prayer. "God hath set eternity in our hearts, and only in Eternity can we reach our full development."[2]

- *The Messiah:* In the Jewish tradition, the Messiah is a human redeemer sent by God to lead the people into a time of unity and peace. At the end of the messianic age, the World to Come begins, together with an end to history as we know it. It is significant that part of this scenario is the resurrection of the dead. The idea that those who yearned for better times will be able to live again and rejoice is perhaps the ultimate source of consolation.

Despite all these enticing ideas, there seems to be a modern reluctance to talk about the hereafter. For some people, the questions of life beyond the grave are so confusing and unsettling that they find it easier to avoid them. Many accept without question the answers that received tradition provides. Some use the afterlife as a way to enforce moral behavior: if we do not behave properly in this life, we will be punished in the next. To others, belief in an afterlife represents a psychological crutch, a way of rationalizing or escaping the cruelties and disappointments of life in this world by looking forward to the next one. These reasons for belief, based on fear and unhappiness, are often cited by people who doubt the existence of a hereafter and insist that only one's life here on earth is real and important.

In contrast, I have found in the course of my research for this book that Jewish sources on the afterlife suggest an array of possibilities infused with hope and faith. Beginning with the Bible and continuing through the sacred texts, permission for hope is always granted. It seems to me that the resilience of that hope – for the world, for the future, and for the individual – is an integral part of the Jewish story.

Judaism's story is a tale of migration, of travels from one place to another. God directed Jews on journeys beginning with Abraham, whom God sent to a land that was still undiscovered as far as Abraham was concerned. It is fitting, then, in Jewish tradition that each person's departure from earthly existence is the beginning of a new journey, one whose landscape and destination we cannot know in advance, but one we can anticipate with hope and not fear. This is something that my father the *rebbe* already knew – that the promise of the World to Come is our affirmation that our God is the God of life.

Notes

Chapter 1: The Hebrew Bible

1. Contradictory opinions still prevail about this subject. Among the scholars who question whether such a belief existed prior to the book of Daniel are Robert Martin-Achard, *From Death to Life* (London: Oliver and Boyd, 1960), 189ff; Lloyd R Bailey, Sr., *Biblical Perspectives on Death* (Philadelphia: Fortress Press, Philadelphia, 1979), 4; *The Anchor Bible Dictionary*, vol. 2 (New York: Doubleday, 1992), 108–10; etc. The following do find evidence of resurrection language in the Hebrew Bible: Mitchell Dahood, *Psalms I* (New York: Doubleday, 1965); Dahood, *Psalms II* (1968); Dahood, *Psalms III* (1970); Leonard J. Greenspoon, "The Origin of the Idea of Resurrection" in *Traditions in Transformation: Turning Points in Biblical Faith*, ed. Baruch Halpern and Jon D. Levenson (Winona Lake, Indiana: Eisenbrauns, 1981), 310–11; Francis I. Andersen and David Noel Freedman, eds., *Hosea*, Anchor Bible Series, vol. 24 (New York: Doubleday, 1980), 420–21.

2. J.W. Ribar, "Death Cult Practices in Ancient Palestine." Ph.D. Diss., University of Michigan, 1973, 45–71. See also Elizabeth Bloch-Smith, *Judahite Burial Practices and Beliefs about the Dead* (JSOT Supplement Series 123, Sheffield: 1992), cited in "Death and the Afterlife: The Biblical Silence," by Richard Friedman and S.D. Overton, in *Judaism In Late Antiquity*, Part 4 (edited by A.J. Avery-Peck and Jacob Neusner, Brill: 1999), 141.

3. "Pit" is rendered in Hebrew as *bor* (see Lam. 3:55) or *shahat* (Ps. 49:10). For a full discussion of the various names for Sheol, see Nicholas J. Tromp, *Primitive Conceptions of Death and the Nether World in the Old Testament*, Pontifical Biblical Institute (Rome: 1969), 20ff.

4. Resurrection is not the same as immortality. Immortality is based on a dualism whereby the soul is eternal and the body destructible. Resurrection, by contrast, is holistic: both body and soul will be revived.

5. Mitchell Dahood translates this as an explicit reference to resurrection: "You will make me know the path of life eternal" (Mitchell Dahood, *The Anchor Bible, Psalms*

1–50, Doubleday, 1965). Scholars do not agree on this translation, but the word order here is what is significant.

6. For a fuller treatment of anti-Baal polemic, see Leah Bronner, *The Stories of Elijah and Elisha*, in vol. VI of the Pretoria Oriental Series, ed. A van Selms, Brill, 1968.

7. These arguments are recorded and refuted by Leonard J. Greenspoon in "The Origin of the Idea of Resurrection." In *Traditions in Transformation: Turning Points in Biblical Faith*, ed. Baruch Halpern and Jon D. Levenson, (Winona Lake, IN: Eisenbrauns, 1981), 247–321.

8. John F. A. Sawyer, "Hebrew Words for the Resurrection of the Dead." *Vetus Testamentum* 23 (1973): 218–34.

9. *Ibid.,* 230.

10. Greenspoon, *"Origin of the Idea of Resurrection,"* 254.

11. Mitchell Dahood, *The Anchor Bible: Psalms II, 51–100* (Garden City, NY: Doubleday & Company, 1968), 195.

12. Genesis 41:4, 7 and 21.

13. I Kings 18:27.

14. Genesis 28:16.

15. Genesis 9:24.

16. I Kings 3:15.

17. 2 Kings 4:31.

18. See Psalm 69:29, where the wicked are erased from the book of life, and Isaiah 4:3, where the righteous are inscribed for life in Jerusalem. The mention of a book of life is well attested in the Bible, where it seems to refer to membership within a covenantal community.

19. See Psalm 16:9: "... For thou dost not give me up to Sheol, or let thy godly one see the Pit." See also 17.5. Though they do not use *l-k-ḥ,* they present a similar theme of a reward of nearness to God and avoiding Sheol.

20. For scriptural examples of the desire of the Hebrews for personal vindication, see Jeremiah 31:29–30, in which the prophet declares that only the person who eats sour grapes will have his teeth blunted, and Ezekiel 18:20, stating that children shall not suffer for the sins of the parents.

21. See James Pritchard, *Ancient Near Eastern Text* (ANET) 1955, 437; Robert Martin-Achard, *From Death to Life*, 83–85 on influence of agricultural cults; 188–89 on influence of Persian Zoroastrian religion.

22. See Andersen and Freedman, *Hosea,* 420.

23. For a detailed discussion of the content and structure of the Isaiah apocalypse, see Yehezkel Kaufmann, *Toledot ha-Emunah ha-Yisraelit* [The Religion of Israel], vol. 3 (1), 186ff; Edward Kissane, *The Book of Isaiah* (Dublin: Browne and Nolin, Ltd., 1941), 267, 303; William R. Miller, *Isaiah 24–27 and the Origin of Apocalyptic* (Montana: Scholar's Press, 1976); Paul D. Hanson, *The Dawn of Apocalyptic* (Philadelphia: Fortress Press, 1979), 98ff.

24. *Encyclopedia Biblica*, vol. 7 (Hebrew) (Jerusalem: Bialik Foundation, 1976), 405, s.v. *Refa'im*.

25. I.W. Slotki, in his commentary on Isaiah (London: The Soncino Press, 1949, 121), supports this view, calling Isaiah 26:19 "an antiphonal song on the resurrection of the dead introduced as an answer to the apparently meaningless suffering and sorrow."

26. See 2 Maccabees 7 for reference to persecution of martyrs.

27. Judah J. Slotki, *Daniel, Ezra, and Nehemiah* (London: The Soncino Press, 1951), xiii.

Chapter 2: Early Post-Biblical Literature

1. For further detailed information see R.H. Charles, *Apocrypha and Pseudepigrapha* v.2, (Oxford: Clarendon Press, 1979), and James Charlesworth, ed., *The Old Testament Pseudepigrapha*, v. 1, (Garden City, New York: Doubleday & Company), 1983. The count there is sixty-five books.

2. BT *Bava Batra* 14b–15a, for rabbinic discussion of authorship of biblical books.

3. Mishnah *Yadayim* 2:5.

4. M. *Megillah* 4:8.

5. Louis Ginzberg, "Some Observations on the Attitude of the Synagogue towards the Apocalyptic-Eschatological Writings," *Journal of Biblical Literature*, v. 51 (1922): 126–27.

6. JT *Sanhedrin* 28a.

7. See, for example, BT *Niddah* 16b, referring to Ben Sira 21:23, and BT *Hagigah* 13a, referring to Ben Sira 3:21–22. There are also references in the Jerusalem Talmud.

8. The discussions on this subject can be found in BT *Sanhedrin* 100b and Tosefta *Yadaim* 1:13.

9. The *Book of Esdras 4*, 14:42–47, Charlesworth, vol. 1, 555.

10. "II Maccabees," *Encyclopaedia Judaica* (Jerusalem: Keter Publishing House, 1971), vol. 11, 658.

11. Fragments of the Hebrew manuscript of the Wisdom of Ben Sira were first found in the Cairo Genizah in 1896, with other Hebrew fragments discovered at various times during the twentieth century. In 1977, scholar Moshe Zvi Segal published a complete Hebrew edition of The Wisdom of Ben Sira.

12. *Encyclopaedia Judaica,* vol. 4, 552.

13. Goodspeed describes the style as "obviously propagandistic": see Edgar J. Goodspeed, *The Apocrypha: An American Translation* (New York: Vintage Books, 1959), 443.

14. 2 Macc. 7:9.

15. 2 Macc. 7:14.

16. In medieval literature, the nameless mother is called Hannah and sometimes also Miriam.

17. 2 Macc. 7:22–23.

18. BT *Gittin* 57b.

19. 2 Macc. 6:30.

20. R. H. Charles, *Apocrypha and Pseudepigrapha of the Old Testament,* vol. 1 (Oxford: Oxford University Press, 1913), 518.

21. Wisdom of Solomon 2:23.

22. Wisdom of Solomon 5:13–16.

23. Philo, *The Works of Philo: Complete and Unabridged,* updated ed., Foreword by David Scholer (Grand Rapids: Hendrickson, 1993), 153.

24. See, for example, Mishnah *Pe'ah* 1:1.

25. Jubilees 23:30–31.

26. 4 Macc. 14:5.

27. 4 Macc. 17:12.

28. 4 Macc. 18:23.

29. 1 Enoch 22:9–10.

30. 1 Enoch 51: 2–3.

31. 1 Enoch 51:10.

32. 1 Enoch 46:3–4.

33. 4 Ezra 5:31–40, 8:47.

34. 4 Ezra 7:11; 7:26; 7:32–34.

35. 4 Ezra 7:80.

36. 4 Ezra 7:81–99; the author first lists the seven forms of torment, then the seven orders of reward.

37. 4 Ezra 7:75.

38. 4 Ezra 7:76–77.

39. Charles, *Apocrypha and Pseudepigrapha,* vol. 2, 615ff.

40. 2 Baruch 30: 1–2.

41. 2 Baruch 50: 2–3.

42. 2 Baruch 51:12.

43. Simcha Paull Raphael, *Jewish Views of the Afterlife* (Northvale, NJ: Jason Aronson, Inc., 1994), 111, and Hans Clemens Caesarius Cavallin, *Life After Death* (Lund, Sweden: GWK Gleerup, 1974), 53–54; these passages are reminiscent of Daniel 12:2. See also the Testament of Zebulon 10:2, in which the sixth son of Jacob promises, "I shall rise again in your midst as a leader among your sons, and I shall be glad in the midst of my tribe."

44. Cavallin, *Life After Death,* 53–55.

45. "Apocalyptic Literature," in *Jewish Writings of the Second Temple Period,* ed. Michael E. Stone (Philadelphia: Fortress Press, 1984), 421.

46. Sibylline Oracles, Book 4, lines 181–86.

47. George W. E. Nickelsburg, *Resurrection, Immortality and Eternal Life in Intertestamental Judaism* (Cambridge, MA: Harvard University Press, 1972), 140; see also Raphael, *Jewish Views of the Afterlife,* 141.

Chapter 3 : The Mishnah

1. Although the creation of *midrashim,* the searching out of hidden meanings in biblical texts, has continued to the present, the writings referred to as Midrash in this book are those that have been published as authoritative texts under titles such as *Genesis Rabbah, Exodus Rabbah,* et al.

2. All references to *Avot* (of which there are numerous translations) follow the verse numeration and translation (unless otherwise noted) in Joseph H. Hertz, *Sayings of the Fathers (Pirke Avot)* (Behrman House, 1945).

3. While the form *tehiyah* is not found in the Bible, the root of the word is ḥ-y-h, which, as noted in Chapter 1, 30–32, is an indicator of resurrection in biblical Hebrew.

4. It occurs thirty times, while the term for resurrection is only found four times.

5. Josephus, *Wars of the Jews,* Book 2, 8:2, (Philadelphia: The John C. Winston Company, n.d.).

6. The same idea can be found in *Avot* 3:19: "Everything is foreseen, yet the freedom of choice is given."

7.   Josephus, *Antiquities of the Jews*, Book 18, 1:3. The "immortal vigor" is a Hellenism; Josephus is using Greek concepts to frame the Pharisaic idea of bodily resurrection.

8.   A very full study of the use and significance of the doctrine of resurrection in this context has been carried out by Claudia Setzer, "Resurrection of the Dead as Symbol and Strategy," *Journal of the American Academy of Religion* (69/1), March 2001.

9.   Josephus, *Antiquities of the Jews*, Book 13, 10:5–6.

10. Josephus, *Antiquities of the Jews*, Book 18, 1:4.

11. Josephus, *Wars of the Jews*, Book 2, 8:14.

12. In other words, the Sadducees were responding to the relative sparseness of references to resurrection in the Bible. Some scholars hold that the Sadducees did believe in resurrection, but not that the belief had its origin in the Torah.

13. Josephus, *Antiquities of the Jews*, Book 13, 10:6.

14. Josephus, *Wars of the Jews*, Book 2, 8:11ff.

15. Aside from Josephus, we know very little about the Essenes, except for passing references in Philo and the Roman Pliny, which scarcely discuss their religious beliefs. The Essenes are not mentioned anywhere in talmudic and Jewish sources.

16. Geza Vermes, *The Complete Dead Sea Scrolls in English,* revised edition (London: Penguin Books, 2004), 412–13.

17. 4Q383–91.

18. James H. Charlesworth *et al., Resurrection: The Origin and Future of a Biblical Doctrine* (New York: T & T Clark, 2006), 36.

19. Vermes, *Complete Dead Sea Scrolls,* 611–12. For a fuller treatment of these texts, see C.D. Elledge, *The Bible and the Dead Sea Scrolls* (Atlanta: Society of Biblical Literature, 2005), 127–28.

20. Setzer ("Resurrection of the Dead as Symbol and Strategy," 87) suggests that the doctrine of resurrection is often found alongside statements that endorse God's power and involvement in human affairs, the primacy of Torah and a concern for ultimate justice. Thus, resurrection forms part of a worldview in which the world is just and coherent. There are similar teachings in both the Mishnah and the Talmud.

21. *Shemot Rabbah* 25:3: The manna had the taste of bread for the young, honey for the old, and oil for babies.

22. The term *apikoros,* heretic, comes from the name of the Greek philosopher Epicurus (342–270 B.C.E.), whom the rabbis viewed as preaching hedonism and rejecting the ideas of God's providence and power on earth. The word is also associated with the Hebrew root *f-k-r,* "to be free of restraint," and therefore to be licentious and skeptical.

23. The Tosefta adds to the Mishnah four other categories of persons who will be denied entry to the World to Come: those who reject the yoke of the precepts, those who annul the covenant, those who deliberately interpret Torah in an erroneous manner, and those who spell out the Divine Name.

24. The *Amidah,* also known as "the Eighteen," is recited three times a day by practicing Jews. Thus a belief in resurrection is articulated three times every day.

25. *Avot* 4:29, my translation.

26. *Avot* 2:8.

27. *Avot* 1:13.

28. *Avot* 2:21.

29. *Avot* 4:7.

30. Traditionally, Tractate *Avot* contains five chapters, but a sixth chapter, called *Kinyan Talmud Torah* (The Acquisition of Torah), was added later by Ashkenazic rabbis who read the chapters of *Pirke Avot* on the Sabbaths between Passover and Shavuot and wanted a sixth reading, for the Sabbath before Shavuot, celebrating the giving of the Torah at Sinai.

31. BT *Hagigah* 14b.

32. My translation.

33. For discussion of this issue, see note to *Avot* 6:4 in Philip Blackman, *Mishnayot: Seder Nezikin* (Brooklyn: Judaica Press, 1963), 542.

34. Hyman Goldin, *Ethics of the Fathers* (New York: Hebrew Publishing Company, 1962), 96. See also Leonard Kravitz and Kerry M. Olitzky, *Pirke Avot: A Modern Commentary on Jewish Ethics* (New York: UAHC Press, 1993), 101.

35. *Sifra* 193, Aharei Mot, Parasha 8.

36. Rabbi Elazar was killed by Bar Kokhba after being accused of treason against his own people, but the charge was never proven. See JT *Ta'anit* 4:5.

37. BT *Bava Metzia* 58b: "He who puts his fellow to public shame is considered as though he had shed blood."

38. *Avot de-Rabbi Nathan,* Version B, Chapter 22.

39. *Avot* 4:21.

Chapter 4: The Talmud

1. References to Talmud in this chapter will be to the Babylonian version unless otherwise noted.

2. This warning appears in the Mishnah in *Sanhedrin* 10 and in the Talmud in *Sanhedrin* 90a.

3. Tractate *Sanhedrin*, Babylonian Talmud (London: The Soncino Press, 1987).

4. The citation of a *min* to provide the opposite pole of an argument is a frequent technique in the Talmud. The term *min* (pl. *minim*) is used to denote many different types of people who challenge rabbinic authority, such as Sadducees, who were Jews holding sectarian differences with the rabbis; early Christians; and rebellious Jews who flout Jewish commandments.

5. Gebiha ben Pesisa was not a rabbi but a pious doorkeeper of the Second Temple, who is said to have made an argument for the Hebrews' claim to the Holy Land to Alexander the Great.

6. During the summer months, worshipers insert "He makes the dew fall" in the same paragraph; cf. Isaiah 26:19 in Chapter 1, 34.

7. The same teaching is found in *Berakhot* 15b.

8. While they speak of a final judgment in the days of the Messiah, they also speak of a judgment following an individual's death that results in reward or punishment.

9. The rabbis of the Mishnah had already adopted the idea that an individual's deeds were recorded during his lifetime so that note could be taken of them at a later date: "All your deeds are written in a book" (Mishnah *Avot* 11:1).

10. There are further discussions of *Gan Eden* and *Gehinnom* in midrashic literature outside the Talmud, but we will confine ourselves to the talmudic references.

11. For the reasoning that leads them to this conclusion, see *Berakhot* 34b.

12. *Sotah* 10b. As noted in Chapter 2, 54, the concept of "seven levels of torment" was mentioned in 4 Ezra. We shall see that the scholars of the medieval period went on to develop this concept further. It is notable, though, that centuries before Dante, there was an idea that Hell had multiple dimensions.

13. *Berakhot* 57b, *Hagigah* 13b, *Menahot* 99b.

14. The biblical prooftext for this idea is a verse from Hannah's song in 1 Samuel 2: "God brings down to Sheol and raises up."

15. A. Cohen, *Everyman's Talmud* (London: J.M. Dent & Sons, 1932), 382.

16. See Chapter 8 for a full discussion of the Messiah.

17. The Ten Martyrs were rabbis who were brutally executed by the Romans. Their stories, gleaned from all over the Talmud, are brought together in the Midrash *Eleh Ezkerah* ("These I Will Remember"), which is recited on Yom Kippur, the Day of Atonement.

18. Also in Midrash *Vayikra Rabbah* 4:5.

19. It is unlikely that the appellation "Queen Cleopatra" refers to the Egyptian queen of legend; it may be a corruption or anagram of some other name or description.

20. This is the kind of death described in *Berakhot* 8a as "a kiss."

Chapter 5: Medieval Jewish Philosophy

1. Although Sa'adiah wrote the work in Arabic, its best-known form is the Hebrew translation created in the late twelfth century.

2. *Saadia Gaon: The Book of Beliefs and Opinions,* trans. Samuel Rosenblatt (New Haven: Yale University Press, 1989). This is a reprint of Rosenblatt's 1948 translation of Sa'adiah's book, the first in English.

3. Saadia Gaon, *The Book of Beliefs and Opinions,* 435.

4. Yehuda Halevi, *The Kuzari: In Defense of the Despised Faith,* trans. and annotated by N. Daniel Korobkin (Northvale, NJ: Jason Aronson Inc., 1998), 46. This discussion is taken from Halevi's First Essay, Section 103. The "designated place" in the direct quotation above is *Eretz Yisrael.*

5. Halevi, *Kuzari,* 280 (Fifth Essay, 12:43–47).

6. Maimonides, *Commentary on the Mishnah,* Introduction to *Sanhedrin* 10:3.

7. Paraphrased from Maimonides, *Hakdamot le-Ferush ha-Mishnah (Introductions to Commentary on the Mishnah),* ed. and commentary by Mordechai Dov Rabinowitz (Jerusalem: Mosad Harav Kook, 1969), 126–27. (Passages in this chapter from the same work were translated by the author.)

8. *Ibid.,* 129.

9. The Thirteen Principles are usually referred to in Hebrew as *shelosha asar ikarim.*

10. Maimonides, *Mishneh Torah: Hilkhot Teshuvah, The Laws of Repentance,* trans. Rabbi Eliyahu Touger (New York: Moznaim Publishing Corporation, 1990), 178–80.

11. Joshua Finkel, *Maimonides' Treatise on Resurrection* (New York: American Academy for Jewish Research, 1939), 64–65; Maimonides, *Treatise on Resurrection,* trans. Fred Rosner (New York: Ktav Publishing Company, 1982), 15–16.

12. Rosner, *Treatise on Resurrection,* 32.

13. *Ibid.,* 32–33.

14. This phrase was coined by Neil Gillman; see Gillman, *The Death of Death: Resurrection and Immortality in Jewish Thought,* (Woodstock, VT: Jewish Lights Publishing, 1997), 160.

15. Nahmanides based this idea on *Rosh ha-Shanah* 16b ff.

16. Compare to the names for the underworld the rabbinic sages listed in *Eruvin* 19a. See also Chapter 4, 89.

17. This is a development of ideas found in *Sotah* 10b.

18. Nahmanides, *The Gate of Reward*, trans. Charles B. Chavel (New York: Shilo Publishing House Inc., 1983), 61.

19. *Ibid.*, 81.

20. *Ibid.*, 64.

21. *Ibid.*, 87.

22. Keats used this phrase in an 1819 letter in which he rejected the normative Christian view of the world as a vale of tears: "Call the world if you please 'the vale of soul-making.' Then you will find out the use of the world."

23. Nahmanides, *The Gate of Reward*, 116.

24. *Ibid.*, 111–12. Nahmanides lists Moses as an example of someone with a more elevated soul (supported by the *Shekhinah*) who did not need to eat manna.

25. *Ibid.*, 129.

26. Joseph Albo, *Sefer ha-Ikkarim* (Book of Principles), Vol. 4, Book 2, trans. Isaac Husik (Philadelphia: The Jewish Publication Society, 1946), 283.

27. *Ibid.*, 347.

28. *Ibid.*, 290.

29. See p. 115 above for a full explanation of this concept.

30. Albo, *Book of Principles*, 290.

31. *Ibid.*, 312–13.

Chapter 6: Mysticism

1. Kabbalah literally means "what is received." In its early uses, the word simply means "tradition." As time passed, the term came to be used to refer specifically to the mystical tradition, which is how it is used today.

2. Shimon bar Yohai, a known recluse, lived during the period of Roman rule in the Land of Israel. According to legend, he spent fifteen years hiding from the Romans in a cave in order to study Torah with his son.

3. See Gershom Scholem, *On the Kabbalah and Its Symbolism* (New York: Schocken Books, 1969), 68. The "Tree of Life" is also a symbol for the *sefirah* of *tiferet* ("beauty" or "splendor"), which in turn is a metaphor for the written Torah.

4. *Zohar*, (London: The Soncino Press, 1984), vol. 5, 211. All *Zohar* quotations are from the Soncino edition. They will be cited by volume and "original" page number after each quotation, with a footnote citation to the correct page in Soncino.

5. *Zohar*, vol. 2, 280.

6. *Zohar*, vol. 5, 188.

7. *Zohar*, vol. 2, 357.

8. *Zohar*, vol. 2, 357–58.

9. *Zohar*, vol. 4, 28.

10. *Zohar*, vol. 4, 25–26.

11. This image recalls the original teaching in the Talmud (*Berakhot* 17a) about the radiance of the *Shekhinah*.

12. *Zohar*, vol. 1, 29.

13. Sa'adiah's antipathy to the idea of transmigration of souls might stem from his opposition to the Karaites, whom he denounced as heretics and whose leader, Anan ben David, embraced the doctrine.

14. Aryeh Kaplan, *The Bahir* (Boston: Weiser Books, 1979), 56–57. Subsequent citations of the *Bahir* will be to Kaplan's translation of the text. While the early kabbalists and some subsequent scholars attribute *Sefer ha-Bahir* to the *tanna* R. Nehunya ben ha-Kana, others find no evidence of such authorship.

15. *Ibid.*, 71.

16. *Ibid.*, 77.

17. *Zohar*, vol. 3, 303. The reference to the "redeemer" is to the biblical *levir*, the brother of the childless man (Deut. 25).

18. *Zohar*, vol. 3, 302.

19. *Zohar*, vol. 2, 216.

20. *Zohar*, vol. 1, 324.

21. See Gershom Scholem, *On the Mystical Shape of the Godhead* (New York: Schocken Books, 1991), 211–12.

22. *Zohar*, vol. 2, 21–22, corresponding to Hebrew *Zohar* vol. 2, 131a.

23. See Fine, *Physician of the Soul, Healer of the Cosmos: Isaac Luria and His Kabbalistic Fellowship* (Stanford, CA: Stanford University Press, 2003), 144, and Gershom Scholem, *Major Trends in Jewish Mysticism* (New York: Schocken Books, 1954), 279.

24. See David Wexelman, *The Jewish Concept of Reincarnation and Creation: Based on the Writings of Rabbi Chaim Vital* (Northvale, NJ: Jason Aronson, 1999), 3–12, for a fuller discussion of the four worlds and the five levels of the soul. The latter are

commonly known among students of Jewish mysticism as NaRaNHY, an acronym (going from lowest to highest) for *nefesh, ruah, neshamah, hayah,* and *yehidah.*

25. Hayyim Vital, *Sha'ar ha-Gilgulim* (Jerusalem: Keren Hotsaath Sifre, 1998), 1–49. For an English translation of the text, see *Sha'ar ha-Gilgulim,* trans. Yitzchak Bar Chaim (Malibu, CA: Thirty Seven Books Publishing, 2003), or see Wexelman for an adapted translation.

26. The practice of full prostration faded in most Jewish communities. Contemporary Orthodox Jews, for example, remain seated, bending the arm that is not wearing *tefillin* on the table in front of them, and resting their foreheads on their arms.

27. Fine, *Physician of the Soul,* 241.

28. Wexelman, *Jewish Concept of Reincarnation,* 8.

29. Kabbalah also brings the 613 commandments into play with references to God's formation of human anatomy: man's 248 "limbs" represent the positive commandments, and his 365 sinews represent the prohibitions. Fulfilling each of the 613 commandments would enable a person to transform his body into a dwelling place for the *Shekhinah.* However, the omission to perform any commandment would require a person to reincarnate over and over again until perfection was achieved.

30. Wexelman, *Jewish Concept of Reincarnation,* 115–16.

31. *Ibid.,* 118.

32. Scholem, *On the Mystical Shape of the Godhead,* 222. He gives the examples of Judah's soul entering that of Boaz and the souls of Aaron's sons, Nadav and Avihu, entering that of Pinhas.

33. *Ibid.,* 213.

34. Hayyim Vital, *Sha'ar Ruah ha-Kodesh,* ed. Yehudah Ashlag (Tel Aviv: Eshel, 1961), 39–40. Cf. Fine, *Physician of the Soul,* 325.

35. Fine, *Physician of the Soul,* 334. See also *Sefer ha-Hezyonot* ("Book of Visions"), ed. Moses Faierstein (Jerusalem: State of Israel Department of Education, Culture and Sport, 2006), 140–42.

36. *Sefer ha-Hezyonot,* 18.

37. Hayyim Vital, Introduction to *Sha'ar ha-Hakdamot.* This essay is generally included in printed editions of Vital's *Etz Hayyim.*

38. Fine, *Physician of the Soul,* 98.

39. Wexelman, *Jewish Concept of Reincarnation,* 111.

40. Fine, *Physician of the Soul,* 326.

41. Over 100,000 Polish Jews were murdered in this uprising of Ukrainian Cossacks under their leader, Bogdan Chmielnicki.

42. This individual, named Ghazzati (c.1644–1690) was the main theologian of the messianic movement of the time, and his opinion carried some weight.

43. Rachel Elior, quoted in Fine, *Physician of the Soul*, 5.

44. David Sears, *The Path of the Ba'al Shem Tov* (Northvale, NJ: Jason Aronson Inc., 1997), 213.

45. Rabbi Nahman of Bratslav, "The Rabbi's Son," in *Nahman of Bratslav: The Tales*, trans. Arnold J. Band (Mahwah, NJ: Paulist Press, 1978), 133–38.

Chapter 7: Modernity

1. One of the first prominent figures of the Jewish Enlightenment was Moses Mendelssohn (1729–1786), an observant Jew who nevertheless moved easily in German intellectual circles.

2. Gillman, *The Death of Death*, 198.

3. Early Reformers favored the approach of keeping the traditional wording in Hebrew but reinterpreting these expressions in their translations.

4. The furor over the 1945 siddur's many excisions and emendations to the traditional liturgy, including the deletion of references to resurrection, culminated in the Union of Orthodox Rabbis expelling Mordecai Kaplan. It was also controversial within the Conservative Jewish Theological Seminary, where Kaplan taught.

5. Gillman, *The Death of Death*, 206.

6. United Synagogue of Conservative Judaism, *Emet v'Emunah*, 29–30.

7. *The Hirsch Siddur* (Jerusalem: Feldheim, 1969), 133.

8. *The Complete Artscroll Siddur*, trans. and commentary by Rabbi Nosson Scherman (Brooklyn: Mesorah Publications, 1987), 99–100.

9. *The Authorised Daily Prayer Book of the United Hebrew Congregations of the British Empire*, commentary by J. H. Hertz (London: Shapiro, Vallentine & Co., 1955), 255.

10. *Ketubbot* 12:3, 35b.

11. Such scholars include the Modern Orthodox thinker Eliezer Berkovitz; Louis Jacobs, associated with the British Masorti movement; Neil Gillman, professor of Jewish philosophy at the Conservative Jewish Theological Seminary; and Eugene Borowitz, a leading theologian in the Reform movement.

12. New York: CCAR Press, 2007.

13. David Posner, "Soul Minders," *Reform Judaism*, Spring 2007, 86.

14. Jon D. Levenson, *Resurrection and the Restoration of Israel: The Ultimate Victory of the God of Life* (New Haven: Yale University Press, 2006), 200.

15. I. L. Peretz, "Three Gifts," trans. by Hillel Halkin, in *The I. L. Peretz Reader*, ed. Ruth R. Wisse (New York: Schocken Books, 1990), 222–30.

Chapter 8: The Messiah

1. Later scholars refer to these troubled times as "the birth pangs of the Messiah."

2. See Amos 9:14–15: "I will restore my people Israel . . . . I will plant them upon their soil / And they will not be uprooted again / From upon the soil that I have given them."

3. References to Elijah in this role appear repeatedly in Jewish liturgy. The Passover *Haggadah* has made it a concept familiar to most Jews, who are instructed to pour a cup of wine for Elijah and to open the door for the prophet during the seder. If he enters, it is a sign that the Messiah is on his way.

4. Seven of the sixty-five pseudepigraphal books contain references. The Book of Jubilees, The Assumption of Moses, and The Testaments of the Twelve Patriarchs all contain material that refers to a messianic age but do not portray a personal Messiah. By contrast, 1 Enoch, the Psalms of Solomon, the Book of Baruch, and 4 Ezra all contain legends woven around the personality of the Messiah.

5. James H. Charlesworth, *The Old Testament Pseudepigrapha*, vol. 1 (Garden City, NY: Doubleday, 1983), 34.

6. 1 Enoch 71:14–16, Charlesworth, *Old Testament Pseudepigrapha*, vol. 1, 50.

7. See Geoffrey Dennis, *The Encyclopedia of Jewish Myth, Magic and Mysticism* (Woodbury, MN: Llewellyn Publications, 2007), 81.

8. JT *Ta'anit* 4:8. Another rabbi, Yohanan ben Torta, immediately counters Akiva's claim, saying: "Grass will grow on your cheeks before the Messiah comes."

9. This is identified with the wars of Gog and Magog (Ezekiel 38).

10. A favorite occupation of the *amoraim* was to discuss who the Messiah would be and what he would be called, with the name denoting his role as redeemer. *Sanhedrin* 98b contains a description of scholars offering praise to their teachers by proposing their names or forms of their names as names for the Messiah, with textual support from the Bible. For example, we find students of Rabbi Shela asserting that the Messiah will be named Shilo, citing Genesis 49:10, "until Shilo comes," as a prooftext, while the school of Rabbi Yannai, citing Psalms 72:17, alleges he will be called Yinnon, and followers of Rabbi Haninah, quoting Jeremiah 16:13, state that the Messiah will bear their teacher's name. In the same Talmud passage, other scholars propose Menahem ("comforter") as the best name for the Messiah, citing

the verse from Lamentations: "Because far from me is a comforter, a reliever of my soul." Additionally, one rabbi proposes that if the Messiah turns out to come from among the living, Rabbi Judah ha-Nasi would be that person, with Daniel as a model if the Messiah arises from the dead; others suggest that he will be another David. Meanwhile, Rabbi Nahman, a scholar of great power and prestige, suggests that he himself might make a good Messiah.

11. See, for example, *Rosh ha-Shanah* 11a.

12. See also the discussion at BT *Sanhedrin* 97a.

13. BT *Sanhedrin* 98a, 663.

14. Maimonides, *The Code of Maimonides: The Book of Judges,* trans. Abraham M. Hershman (New Haven: Yale University Press, 1949), 239–40. The biblical quotation is Zephaniah 3:9.

15. *Ibid.,* 240.

16. Nahmanides, *Kitvei Rabbenu Moshe ben Nahman,* ed. Charles Chavel (Jerusalem: Mosad ha-Rav Kook, 1963), 310–11, as quoted in *Encyclopaedia Judaica,* vol. 6, 93.

17. This understanding came about as a result of interpreting the letters that make up the word for man – *adam* – as denoting, respectively, Adam, David, and the Messiah. See Vital, *Sha'ar ha-Gilgulim,* 284, and the translation by Yitzchak Bar Chaim, 310, for a detailed chronology of the transmigration of Adam's soul from one biblical and rabbinic personage to another.

18. *Encyclopaedia Judaica,* vol. 10, 618–19.

19. Arthur Green, *A Guide to the Zohar* (Stanford, California: Stanford University Press, 2004), 153–54.

20. Borowitz, *Renewing the Covenant,* (Philadelphia: Jewish Publication Society, 1991), 201–2.

21. Tzvi Hirsch Kalischer, *Drishat Tziyon,* ed. Yisrael Klausner (Jerusalem: Mosad HaRav Kook, 1972), 88.

22. Citing the Talmud, Rabbi Teitelbaum claimed that a Jewish state would violate three oaths listed in *Ketubbot* 111a: that Israel shall not "go up by a wall" [return to the Land of Israel by force], that Israel shall not rebel against the nations of the world, and that idolaters "shall not oppress Israel too much."

23. In fact, at the pace of a strolling donkey, as depicted in Zechariah 9:9: "Your king is coming to you . . . humble, riding on an ass, on a donkey foaled by a she-ass."

24. For a fuller discussion, see Rabbi Aaron Soloveitchik, "Israel's Day of Independence: Reflections in Halacha and Hashkafa." *Gesher* (student publication of Rabbi Isaac Elchanan Theological Seminary, Yeshiva University) 4/1 (1969).

25. Quoted in David Ariel, *What Do Jews Believe?* (New York: Schocken Books, 1995), 244.

Afterword

1. Adapted from *The Authorised Daily Prayer Book of the United Hebrew Congregations of the British Empire*, Commentary by J.H. Hertz (London: Shapiro, Vallentine & Co., 1955), 19. The prayer's text is taken from the BT *Berakhot* 60b.
2. *Ibid.*, 255.

Index

About the Author

Dr. Leila Leah Bronner is a noted author, professor, writer, and community activist.

Born in Czechoslovakia to hasidic parents who fled to the United States shortly before the outbreak of World War II, Dr. Bronner grew up in New York, where she received her early education. After marrying, she and her husband, Rabbi Joseph Bronner, moved to South Africa, where she continued her academic education while raising three children and became the first woman in South Africa to receive a doctorate in Ancient Semitic Languages and History.

Dr. Bronner served as Professor of Bible and Jewish History at Witwatersrand University in Johannesburg until her return to the United States. Settling in Los Angeles, she has served as an adjunct associate professor of Jewish history at the University of Judaism and as a visiting scholar at Harvard University, Bar Ilan University in Israel, and Yeshiva University's Institute of Adult Studies in New York.

A strong proponent of the idea that women should have access to all Jewish texts and to higher Jewish learning, Dr. Bronner has been an active member of the Jewish Orthodox Feminist Alliance since its formation in the late 1990s and participated in several of its conferences. In South Africa, the clearest legacy of her interest in women's education is the Leila Bronner Girls High School, named in her honor.

Dr. Bronner's books and articles focus on the Hebrew Bible, other religious writings, themes in Jewish history and culture, and women's issues. Her published books include: *Eve to Esther: Rabbinic Reconstructions of Biblical Women*, which received a Literary Achievement Award from B'nai Zion Western Region, *Stories of Elijah and Elisha, Sects and Separatism During the Second Jewish Commonwealth, Biblical Personalities and Archaeology,* and *Stories of Biblical Mothers: Maternal Power in the Hebrew Bible*. She currently resides in Los Angeles and devotes much of her time to teaching and writing.